Becoming Gods

Interdimensional Mind
Earth Changes and The Quickening
UFO's Their Origins and Intentions

Cazekiel
as received by
James Gilliland

Table of Contents

In Appreciation

Thanks go to all my friends and students/teachers at the Self-Mastery Earth Institute and all those who chose to heal, evolve and gain from the teachings in the first book.

I thank the Beautiful Many Angelic Guides, Ascended Masters and other spiritually advanced beings from the Andromedas, Pleiades/Plejaran and Orion systems who helped me to unlock and understand the mysteries of the universe, our ancient ancestors and UFOs, their origins and intentions.

I also want to acknowledge my Earth Masters from Tibet, India and Asia, and a grand old lady called Nature.

My greatest appreciation is to the God within you which led you to this book—and the beginning of an outrageous adventure into Interdimensional Mind.

Enjoy in love and light,
James Gilliland

Preface

The purpose of this book is to bring understandings to Humanity and the Earth in preparation for exciting times of tumultuous social, economic and physical Earth changes. It is also to prepare you for a grand reunion with your ancient ancestors, the star nations and the very God of your being.

These understandings are necessary for enlightenment, which means to be in knowledge of the whole truth—both sides of the coin. Knowing the truth of your past, which has made you what you are today, will break the spell of forgetfulness and allow ancient memories to come forward. Knowledge and memories have been suppressed lifetime after lifetime. This is the place where all the pieces of the puzzle come together for courageous souls who desire to wake up, remember their Divinity and their ancient origins, regain their power and take a quantum leap in consciousness.

Those who desire to remain in their comfort zones and social consciousness, clinging to the recycled ignorance of the past—the religious dogma, scientific dogma, superstitious beliefs and perpetuated half truths—will struggle with these understandings. Yet one by one as these understandings begin to unfold, as truth always does, the struggle will give way to enlightenment. It is unavoidable in the days to come.

May unconditional love, joy, peace, individual freedom and prosperity reign supreme. May this be a tool to get you there.

Cazekiel

Foreword

When I first went to the sanctuary at Trout Lake, Washington on August 17th, 2006, I had long suspected that UFO's existed, but had never seen one myself. Of course, I wanted to see one. I had heard for many months that perhaps the best place in the country to have this experience was at the retreat owned by James Gilliland. What was about to happen was well beyond my imagination and transformed me into a new and enlightened being with more love inside of me than I knew existed.

I actually had been invited to come to James' as a guest speaker for the Science, Spirit, and Earth Transformation Conference that weekend. I had written a national best seller on the creation of the Earth with my co-author EJ Clark that gave me a small amount of notoriety, so I felt honored to be asked to share my ideas.

Over the next few days, I had amazing experiences that opened me and expanded my view of the universe more than you can know. And yes, I did have my first UFO sighting. I know you want to know more about that, but we'll save that for another time and place.

When James allowed me to review this book, *Becoming Gods II*, there was a great sense of anticipation. As one of my teachers, and one of the most charitable and merciful persons I have ever known, I knew that what James had written in this book would be powerful. I have not been disappointed. There is great work done between its covers.

The challenge of awakening human beings to the fact that they're an eternal entity having mortal experiences is overwhelming at times.

The vast majority of people go through life asleep. They punctuate their lives with paydays or family vacations or even holiday events. The rest of the time they are simply going through the motions of life, but not really experiencing the full purpose of life. In fact, they may have no clue about the purpose of life.

Some people are awake, and besides their constant state of amazement, they feel compelled to reach out and help others to realize there is much more to life than the solids to which we can become so attached. That is where the value of this book is made plain. You can search the world and read volumes of reference material. You can visit the masters in Tibet, or practice Yoga, or attend any workshop you like. But, **you will not get more information about the nature of Earth or the human entity than by reading this book.** Read with an open mind and try to visualize the teachings one by one, and you will see that they are true.

Is the planet Earth hollow? Is there life before birth and after death? Is there a reason why people fall in love? Are there really such a things as soul mates? Is it possible that the Earth itself is a living thing? Are there other dimensions that contain teachers and masters who are willing to help us ascend and transcend our carnal natures and become what we were designed to be? Is it possible that we are gods ourselves? These questions and much, much more are answered with full intention in this book.

All I ask is that you give this your attention. When you're finished, tell a friend and pass along the awareness you now have.

Peace, Earth explorers,
Brooks A. Agnew, PhD
Host of X-Squared Radio

From the Heart of a Prophet

After my near death experience, I received a gift of what can only be referred to as Interdimensional Mind. It did not come all at once. I had to work at it. It was as if a door had opened, but I had to discipline myself to continuously walk through it.

I began to have experiences and receive teachings, which upon returning to this dimension caused me to rearrange my consciousness. I had to let go of many primitive and superstitious beliefs and a lot of fear and feelings of unworthiness.

Cazekiel was the first during my near death experience to cradle me in his golden white light of pure, unconditional love and joy; "Bliss." I found later he was referred to by other grand Masters as the God of Eternal Bliss, which definitely went along with my experience.

Cazekiel expanded my consciousness in several subsequent white light experiences, one of which was so expansive I gazed back upon the Earth only to see what looked like an emerald grain of sand. It took me two weeks to get my feet back on the ground and bring things back into full focus in this reality. Even after that experience, I still had fears concerning other spirits. I figured anyone else but Jesus was a spook.

My fears were honored, and Jesus began to appear in my dreams and meditations. This must be an immense babysitting job, because so many orthodox religions have set it up so he—and only he—must appear to so many, ignoring a whole host of other Angelic Guides and Ascended Masters.

After years of receiving guidance and teachings from within, Jesus appeared one day, arm in arm with another wonderful Master named Baba Ji, who is often referred to as the Yogi Christ. I figured any friend of Jesus is a friend of mine, and Baba Ji began to balance out my understandings concerning Eastern thought.

I also experienced Buddha along the way and even had a conversation with Mohammed. I found the consciousness and energy of each Master to be similar. They each delivered the same message in their own unique way, and I found that they often focused or had a little more expertise in one area or another. If one was better suited to teach or heal what was necessary in the moment, the others graciously stepped aside.

Just as I was feeling comfortable with my studies in Eastern thought, Jesus appeared again with another Ascended Master named White Eagle. This began my teachings in Native American beliefs, which again incorporated the same basic principles and understandings. There was a little more emphasis on the sacredness of all life, and a deep love and respect for the Earth.

One day during a meditation after the medicine wheel, I looked up, only to see Jesus presiding over the circle, hands outstretched, sending love and healing to all who would accept it. This finally drove home the message once and for all. After whacking myself in the forehead with my hand so I wouldn't forget, I blurted out, "It doesn't matter." A few people looked at me in confusion and I repeated, "It just doesn't matter." God is multilingual; a call to spirit is heard no matter how it is made. The only thing that matters is your integrity and your goals and intentions.

A grand revelation came to me. The names, images and doctrines have only created separation, division and war. Each Master had a deep and profound love for God, Humanity and Nature. Where did all this other stuff come from if there are no divisions in God and no separation in omnipresence? If in spirit there is peace and harmony, and they all agree, what happened here on Earth? Man is what happened, and man's struggle for power and control.

In ignorance, man has created primitive and superstitious beliefs which have left a long legacy of separation, division and war. The belief that God is separate from the rest of Humanity in all its cultural diversity, and Nature, has brought great suffering to Humanity and Nature. It has also lined the pockets of some very rich men, who in their unbridled greed and lust for power care nothing for Humanity and Nature. They are the ones who are perpetuating the beliefs in separation and division.

It's time to wake up. Every Master that ever walked this plane had a deep and profound love for God, Humanity and Nature. We can no longer afford the luxury of continuing to support beliefs which continue to perpetuate separation, division and war, or act in any way against Humanity and Nature.

Rather than blame or give credit to wrathful Gods and tormenting devils, now is the time for accountability and responsibility for one's attitudes, emotions, actions and beliefs, which govern our tomorrow individually and collectively. We must cease defending names, images, doctrines and borders, transcend cultural and religious boundaries, and focus mainly on the similarities, not the differences.

There are Universal Principles and understandings found throughout all cultures and beliefs. We are more than our personalities and our bodies. We are multidimensional beings existing on a vibrational continuum expanding in consciousness into higher states of pure, unconditional love, joy, power and wisdom; "Bliss."

We are one race; we share one planet, and are all divine born of the original light. We are Gods. We have brothers and sisters throughout the universe, and we are on a journey and a process that is taking us home, a place where all dimensions and all life come together.

In service to the most high,
James

1

Journey Into Christ Consciousness

I Am Cazekiel

I am Cazekiel, God of eternal bliss. Who I am is unimportant. Who you are, where you are and where you are going are of greater importance.

I am neither higher nor lower than one of you. What I am is an example of your true nature, your God nature. The only difference between you and the greatest of all Gods is different levels of forgetfulness.

I and an unseen brotherhood are here once again in numbers and consciousness like never before in the history of Humanity. We are here to remind you of your Divinity, your true heritage and a journey you have chosen into the Christ Consciousness. It is our purpose to assist Humanity to understand, assimilate and flow with the new Higher Consciousness and Energy, which is creating radical changes in the lands, as well as in consciousness.

You are all being lifted into a greater sensitivity, a greater awareness of other planes, dimensions and those who reside upon them. In truth, you are much more than your body and personality. The one consciousness that encompasses all consciousness on all planes and all dimensions is within you. You are a multidimensional being existing on a vibrational continuum expanding into higher states of pure, unconditional love, joy, power and wisdom into the very Source of all life.

May you be one with creation, as we are one. These understandings are designed to show you where you have been, where you are now and where you are going.

Let the journey begin.

A Cazekiel Truth

Truth is always unfolding, yet along with a great explosion of light and knowledge comes a lot of debris, often consisting of religious dogma, scientific dogma, superstitious beliefs and reality as it is now seen. **In the days to come, there will be many truths unfolding from many planes, many dimensions and through many prophets, channels and visionaries.**

There are many levels of existence to the human experience, and planets also have separate realities. If you were to go to a planet in your third dimensional body and find no life and return in your etheric body in what would seem like a dream, there may exist a whole civilization. On their level, you may or may not be real. Everything is physical to the civilization existing on that level; yet to your level, it would be nonphysical once you return to your physical reality.

Many truths will also come from other civilizations which reside far off in some distant galaxy, with their perspective mixed in with the perspective of the chosen one on the Earth delivering their truth. It is often altered and boxed into the receiver's present belief system, yet they are delivering the messages to the best of their ability. The process involves filtering the messages through their own consciousness, which is necessary to bring it into this plane of understanding. Not only does truth depend upon the clarity of the one receiving the information, it also depends upon the level one is receiving information from and the intentions of the one from which they are receiving the information.

These truths will concern the origin and destiny of man, and many will take credit or blame others for many fortu-

---

nate and less fortunate events. There will be hierarchies and "lowarchies" (you will probably be in the "lowarchy") and many grand events that are going to either save or destroy you in the future. There will be religious truths, scientific truths, metaphysical truths, historical truths, your governments' truths, manufactured consensus where often noble people are discredited or demonized by gossip and rumors through the media, and a whole host of other truths which will rise and fall as time marches onward.

Truth will always be evolving. Yesterday's theories, which became today's facts, often become tomorrow's ignorance. So what is true? It all depends upon your reference point and your perspective. There is black history, white history, yellow history, red history, and it is all different according to the reference point of the one recording the event.

> *Truth will always be evolving.*

There is even the female perspective and the male perspective. As this barrage of truth comes forward, it will get very confusing. So what does one do amidst all the confusion? **It is going to be imperative that each individual develops a nondefensive, nonjudgmental attitude and allows others their truth.** It is also important to develop your own inner sensitivity and feeling nature to discern what is true for you.

If a truth steers you away from your Divinity, let it go. If you are living in the past and that past is filled with bitterness and againstness and does not bring you joy, release it. If a truth does not honor the powerful manifesting God within you, tells you that you are mentally, emotionally, spiritually or genetically incapable of becoming one with GOD, or demands subservience to a higher authority somewhere outside of self, ignore it. If a truth is riddled with images of wrathful Gods and tormenting devils in which to place blame or to give credit, releasing you from accountability and responsibility from your own self-created realities, disempowering you, question it.

If a truth does not lift and empower you, honoring you as a unique expression of GOD with a divine right to free will and self-determination, find another truth. If a truth tells you that you don't have to do anything, that everything will be taken care of by some greater force, I would be highly suspicious of that greater force. There are teachers, healers and grander intelligences that will help you help yourself. They will work with you as long as you are going forward, yet they understand that to tell you how to live your lives and to save you from gaining the wisdom from the experiences your self-created realities bring to you creates devolution, not evolution.

> *If a truth does not lift and empower you... find another truth.*

Now that you have a greater understanding concerning truth, I will give you a Cazekiel truth to run by your own inner authority. *There are a few truths we would like to address, which if you depend upon them in the days to come will cause you a very discomforting experience.*

No one is going to beam you up at the last moment, relieving you of the responsibility to prepare or do anything, so you can continue business as usual. Although there are those in the seen and unseen that have those capabilities, they are bound by what is often referred to as the Prime Directive. After all, what would they do with you? Do you think they would take you to their planet and allow you to do the same to it as Earth? Would they take you to another planet with your competitive warring nature and infect it?

Very few of you have the consciousness to sit in peace with a loving heart without trying to conquer them. Very few would abstain from war, enforcing your beliefs on others rather than using their knowledge for the highest and best good of Humanity and the Earth. The knowledge and power would corrupt you. These grander intelligences will be contacting those with open minds and loving hearts; "the meek." They will inspire you from a distance, and when you are mentally, emotionally and spiritually ready, and when you can meet them on even ground without fear or wanting to worship them, they will make their presence known to you physically, only because you have earned it. You must have the consciousness for it.

Another truth is that you will ascend, levitate, or the rapture will save you. Again, until that time, you can continue business as usual. **If you accept this truth, you are going to have a rude awakening.** There shall come a time when this will happen, yet it will be after the changes. You may ascend after death, when your body descends back into the Earth. You may also levitate when you leave your body under a pile of rubble after the great quakes. The rapture may come 500 feet beneath the water, after a great wave. Your body may ascend back up to the surface, while your spirit goes on to another plane or dimension.

Another very nasty trick some of you are playing upon yourself is thinking "GOD will take care of me," but not if you continue in denial and refuse to listen to even this God who is spelling it out for you. **The God that is going to take care of you is the God within you that is telling you to prepare,** if you want to continue in the physical.

There is the truth that there are alternate realities, and so those who believe that there will be no Earth changes will not experience them. Many also believe that by addressing the Earth changes you create them; and by merely saying it isn't so, the whole universe is going to stop its forward momentum just for them, because they are special. They need a vision beyond their petty denials. The alternate realities do exist, yet you are presently expressing on this frequency in a physical body on the physical body of Earth.

The reality you are expressing upon now has a destiny. It can be altered, yet many of the changes are necessary to balance and heal the planet. To be enlightened is to be aware of that destiny, why the changes are necessary, and what changes are necessary to heal the planet and be supportive of the Earth's needs. Pray for the best concerning Humanity and the Earth, and prepare for changes in the lands as well as in consciousness. **You are entering exciting times of tumultuous change.**

Lovingly and joyously unite and prepare. Do it in love of self, Humanity and the Earth, not in fear. The prophets and visionaries can alter destiny by reaching enough people to redirect their thoughts and actions. Listen to them, run it by your own inner guidance, and make any adjustments you deem necessary.

Still another truth is concerning a great light that is coming in your future, and a band of energy being placed around your planet which is vibrational lifting and is increasing the frequency and vibration of the Earth, and your bodies as well. There is a lot of clarification in this area. **There are many truths concerning this event.** There are many groups taking credit for it and many explanations concerning how it works, and how it is going to affect you and the planet. **We are going to simplify it.** It is not that complicated, nor is it as bizarre as many have described it. You know how that is—the more bizarre, the more names and images of lords, masters and hierarchies, beastly civilizations, etc., the more complex, the more copies it sells.

Although there are a lot of wonderful beings and spiritually and technologically advanced civilizations connected to this event, and a divine science is unfolding, do not get lost in names, images, civilizations or hierarchical orders. In other words, do not get so distracted and far out that you forget your own Divinity and your own healing and awakening. You are also GOD taking a stroll in the physical, and you must do your part in this drama.

This great light and the band of energy can be easily understood when you understand the nature of Higher Consciousness and Energy. Everything begins in consciousness. As consciousness is lowered in vibration, it becomes light. As the light is lowered, it becomes energy. When energy is lowered once again, it becomes mass. In other words, your body is coagulated thought.

It is best to see your body more as condensed consciousness. Your physical body is the by-product of an energy body, which is the by-product of a light body, which is the by-product of pure consciousness that extends into forever, or higher, more expanded states of consciousness.

See your body as condensed consciousness.

The last frontier of identity is often referred to as your God self. It is a vibrational continuum. In truth, as we have said before, **you are a multidimensional being existing on a vibrational continuum.** Along this continuum you have a physical body, a mental body, an emotional body, an astral body, an etheric body (which is the soul or the perfect whole and healthy incarnation), and other higher bodies referred to as the Christ self and the even more expanded God self. **What is happening is an invasion of the God self down through this vibrational continuum all the way to the physical. THIS IS THE BIG PICTURE.** There are a lot of other little pictures in between.

When the frequency of Earth increases, the frequency of your body also increases. This increase raises the vibration of the Earth body, and your body as well. The Earth and you start moving towards an energy body. You become more sensitive and aware of other planes and dimensions, some of which have existed right alongside of you and have always been aware of your existence.

Thought also has a vibration, and as we mentioned earlier, mass is nothing more than coagulated thought. **The lower vibrational thoughts such as fear, guilt, anger, greed, againstness, jealousy, etc., are being vibrationally lifted or amplified** in this process. The Earth body and your physical bodies are filled with these lower vibrational attitudes and emotions to one degree or another. As the vibrational lifting continues, these lower vibrational attitudes and emotions will surface to be released and healed. This process is no longer an option; everyone is along for the ride. This is happening with the entire planet, and all physical life on the planet.

The vibrational lifting and healing process is occurring within your mental body, your emotional body and your astral body. This explains why there is so much turmoil and confusion on every level. **All of the wounds, traumas and wrong conclusions from past experiences are surfacing to be healed within these four lower bodies.**

The Earth is cleansing, healing and releasing all coagulated thought of a lower vibrational nature. She is addressing the areas where the consciousness of the past has psychometrized into the land, due to wars and other actions against Humanity and Nature. She is also going to address the lands in the present which are continuing in this behavior. The ruins of ancient civilizations which have been cleansed in the past will rise again beneath your oceans, and areas where the land has not been defiled will remain. Water has always been a great cleanser.

Your physical bodies will undergo many changes as they release and heal the lower vibrational attitudes and emotions which have coagulated within them. This is the origin of disease, which many enlightened doctors are starting to discover. All disease begins with an unresolved or unhealed attitude or emotion creating an energy imbalance which diminishes or disrupts the natural flow of energies. This includes the attitudes and emotions of your lineage which you inherited as genetic cellular memory. This too will surface to be healed.

All disease begins with an unresolved attitude or emotion.

When the cellular memory is released into your auric field, **you will be feeling the attitudes and emotions of your**

---

ancestors. As the new Higher Consciousness and Energy continues to do its work, your bodies will also undergo a genetic alteration and rewiring, so to speak. This will be necessary to assimilate the new Higher Consciousness and Energy.

The lower vibrational attitudes and emotions in your mental and emotional bodies, when vibrationally lifted and amplified, will surface, and there will be a lot of dramas playing out. Individually and collectively, people will project these unhealed or unresolved issues upon others. They will manifest and magnetize people and events into their daily lives as divine mirrors and teachers of what resides within self. The action/reaction principle often referred to as karma will also be accelerated. The smart ones will own their experiences as self-created realities, take responsibility and heal their unresolved issues.

You are not only dealing with this life, but past lives as well. As the past life issues begin to surface, deep wounds, traumas and fears will surface; and to some,

> *You are not only dealing with this life, but past lives as well.*

they will have no apparent reason. Nothing in this life can attribute to the feelings coming forward. **All wrong conclusions from past experiences, karmic ties and unfinished business from past lives will come forward to be healed and released.** These experiences will eventually settle into the soul as wisdom, and it will be finished.

Eventually, the whole and healthy perfect incarnation referred to as the soul or etheric self will manifest, and disease shall be no more. Unconditional love, joy, peace, abundance and individual freedom will be all that is left upon this plane, which brings us back to God, the God of your being. That is how the process works. Too simple? It is that simple. You are entering the age of God. You can make it as difficult, complicated or sensational as you wish.

Another truth is that you are going to be saved by

Jesus, Buddha, Mohammed, The Great White Spirit or Brotherhood, or some Cosmic Event that will fix everything. Again, like before, you can continue business as usual.

WAKE UP! **You will save all of us a lot of work and frustration if you would listen to the God within you, take responsibility and save yourselves.** This is your reality, your creation, and the re-actions to your actions. You are all powerful manifesting Gods walking through your own creations individually and collectively. Accountability, responsibility and integrity are in order. We are here to inspire you and help you remember your Divinity.

We are not here to save you. We are here to lend you some energy and inspire you to save yourselves. We are here again, as we have been before in times of great changes in the lands, as well as in consciousness. Those who heed the warnings and prepare spiritually, mentally, emotionally and physically will be the seed people for a new age, an age referred to as the Golden Age of GOD.

There is a lot of work to do. It is going to be done along *with* you, not *for* you or *to* you. There will be Divine intervention. It will be as if the whole universe has come to observe and assist in the birth of a people and a planet.

You all have your part to play in this grand event. Keep going forward, be sincere in your commitment, and ask or initiate the awakening and healing process through prayer and meditation. As long as you act upon what is given without denial, selflessly and in the highest and best good of Humanity and the Earth, you will see a grand reunion. A new Earth and a new consciousness will come forward upon the land. Follow your heart and your own inner sensitivity.

> *There is always a lie in be*li*eve. There are always two sides to a coin. Only when the coin is standing on end and you can see both sides can you perceive the whole truth; even then it will probably lean in your direction.*
>
> Cazekiel

So You Want To Be a Christ

There are many who believe that if they were only enlightened, at one with GOD, all of their problems would be solved. Their challenges would be over, and they could live the rest of their lives in bliss. This brings us to the age-old question, "If a tree fell in the forest and nobody was there to hear it, would it make a sound?" If you were a Christ and lived on Earth, would the Earth still have problems?

With an expanded Christ Consciousness, **the Earth and Humanity are you; therefore the Earth's problems and Humanity's problems are yours.** GOD is the one consciousness that encompasses all consciousness, and service to GOD includes Humanity, Nature and life in all its forms on all planes and dimensions. The challenges become greater, yet the access to Higher Consciousness and Energy also becomes available, and you have at your command the wisdom and power to meet these greater challenges.

Before you grab for your robes and set out to heal and conquer the world's problems, there are a few words of caution. There are two sides to the coin. **Being a Christ is not as easy as you think.** Higher Consciousness

Being a Christ is not as easy as you think.

and Energy can be your best friend and your worst foe. **You become a divine mirror, reflecting back everything people love and hate about themselves.** You reflect back to them their iniquities, their lack of self-worth and their shortcomings. People become secretly envious. You become a great amplifier and amplify their fears, insecurities, angers, jealousies, judgments, unresolved issues and old wounds and traumas from past experiences. Rather than look into the mirror and own their reflection, it is often human nature to project, blame and break or do away with the mirror.

The Higher Consciousness and Energy also brings forward any lower vibrational attitudes and emotions within you. This includes cellular memory within your body and any unresolved issues within your mental, emotional and astral bodies where past life issues reside. There is a quickening in your own evolution.

The Christ Consciousness also goes against religious dogma, scientific dogma and the standards set by social consciousness, which will often war upon you or reject you at every turn. There are those who have their images and doctrines, barbaric as they may be, who will judge and condemn you if you do not measure up to their image. The doctrines are often in the name of GOD or Jesus (who gave stern warnings concerning judgment and condemnation). They arrogantly have put themselves above the Angelic Guides and Ascended Masters, professing to know what is best for each soul in ignorance of knowing what is needed within that soul for completion.

If that were not enough, **there are many glorified egos that will try to improve or exalt their status at your expense. What better trophy than to bag or take down a Christ?** If you will look back in your history, prophets and saints die young. Their careers are always shortened by pompous and arrogant men who are secretly jealous and envious and are threatened by their talents and abilities, especially when it threatens beliefs, power and positions.

There is one other thing we might mention, and that is the fact that there are very few mirrors to support and reflect back to you who you truly are. The only place, in most cases, you can truly experience your Divinity is in nature or seclusion. Why do you think every Master spent long hours away from society? It is to step out of social consciousness and remember. You become a stranger in your own land, in the world but not of it, an alien, so to speak.

So why do it? Why on Earth would anyone want to be a Christ? I will tell you why. **First and foremost is because your brothers and sisters need you.** They need to look into a mirror that breaks the spell of social consciousness. The future of Humanity and the Earth depends on you. GOD is depending on you. GOD has sent his best—the bravest of Angels—to become divine mirrors and vibrational bridges for the Christ Consciousness, the mind of GOD.

There are a few bennies that come with the Christ Consciousness we haven't told you about. **One benefit is a wonderful gift called Interdimensional Mind, and the wonderful experiences that come with it.** The Kingdom of GOD has many planes and dimensions, with beautiful beings existing within them. You also become one with the Beautiful Many Saints, Sages, Angelic Guides and Ascended Masters. You are never alone. **All you need to do is but ask, and you can receive** love feedings, power feedings, guidance and help in your endeavors upon the Earth. The greatest gift of all is access to the unconditional love, joy, power and wisdom of the very Source itself.** Rather than reacting to the world, you will become lord over mass, and manifest your own destiny. You will come to realize and be what you have been all along, yet this time you will be awake. You will realize that you have been at the helm of your own ship from the beginning.

> *All you need to do is but ask, and you can receive love feedings, power feedings, guidance and help.*

It is an arduous journey that takes a brave soul with a steadfast conviction, but the perks are worth it. It is a treasure that is beyond value, eternal and well worth the trials and tribulations.

There is nothing worth the Christ Consciousness. No castle, no amount of gold or jewelry, no Earthly position can compare to the kingdom of the Christ. Reason this: If you could manifest all that you desire from pure thought, why settle for the trinkets? If you were offered three wishes, an enlightened one would ask to be the grantor of those wishes and have the power to manifest.

For those who desire to begin this journey, here are a few tips concerning the unfoldment of the Christ Consciousness. We spoke earlier about having to go against the accepted standards of society, with all of its religious and scientific dogmas. There are also those whose positions and security are dependent upon the continuation of this limited consciousness. It is a flaw within the collective consciousness to resist change and fear the unknown, which you represent. Sound familiar?

So what do you do when they judge and condemn you, ridicule you, betray you and war upon you? You first love, bless and forgive yourself for creating the experience. This removes you from any victim role and places you back in the driver's seat. **Then allow that blessing to flow through you, to them and the experience, from your being.** It is their truth, their projection, and they can own it. **Forgive them for their ignorance.**

You must learn self-love, self-authority and to set boundaries. Stay centered in your truth. If you judge, argue or war upon others, you have crossed over into their territory and have to play by their rules. In other words, you become just like them, lowering your vibration.

Judging and condemning others hooks you into their energies. Loving unconditionally, allowing them and sending a blessing their way, releases you and amplifies the lower vibrational attitude and emotion on their side of the coin. This quickens the manifestation of the lessons they need to learn.

Remember: The only reason anyone has any power over you is because you want something from them. They hook you because you want their approval, acceptance or love, or you are unsure and have not yet gained a conviction for your own truth, something you must find within yourself. If you have to war over a truth, then you don't own it. Gaining a conviction has nothing to do with their approval or acceptance. Allow them their truth, however limited.

They are correct, because consciousness creates reality, and they have not allowed the reference points to create a grander truth. Love yourself for having the courage to expand beyond social consciousness.

With the Light Comes Responsibility

There is a saying concerning the transference of consciousness and energy to another and the changing of one's ways. It was concerning the casting out of a demon, after which a stern warning was delivered that if the benefactor of the healing did not change his ways, seven more demons would come upon him.

Demons in today's terminology are discarnate spirits, which, due to unresolved issues or unfinished business, are trapped between worlds. They often hook into the consciousness of others of like mind and either possess or influence them. This can include past life influences as well.

Once a person is lifted into a higher state of consciousness, he or she cannot afford to continue old habits, and must discipline his or her self from expressing the lower vibrational attitudes and emotions such as fear, anger, jealousy, etc. **These lower vibrational attitudes and emotions attract discarnate spirits in the astral levels.** One can also inadvertently attune to these same attitudes and emotions within the collective consciousness and within other people in the vicinity, adding to your own process.

Lower vibrational attitudes and emotions attract discarnate spirits.

When one expands in consciousness, he or she takes on greater territory and a responsibility to heal what is within that greater territory. Self-discipline and self-authority are imperative. *The greater sensitivity of an expanding* *consciousness is often accompanied with not only experiencing Angelic Guides, Ascended Masters and other benevolent spirits, but seeing, feeling or hearing lower vibrational influences as well.* It can be very discomforting and unpleasant in the beginning, yet this becomes easier to handle as you grow more proficient in healing.

This is often referred to as multiple personality disorder, schizophrenia or spiritual emergencies. These can be addressed in most cases by acknowledging, understanding and healing any unseen negative influences. Explaining the situation and teaching individuals the tools and techniques to heal themselves, rather than suppressing the experience with drugs, is of greater benefit to the healing process.

Humanity as a collective is being vibrationally lifted into a greater sensitivity and is becoming aware that there is much more to the universe than the physical. Along with this greater sensitivity and awareness, as aforementioned, lies the responsibility to heal any unseen negative influences. These influences have been there all along. The only thing that is changing is the heightened sensitivity and awareness.

Now is the time to take responsibility and learn how to have dominion over the new expanded consciousness. We believe it is imperative to again give these tools and techniques which were given in the first book [*Reunion with Source,* originally titled *Becoming Gods*], due to the necessity and importance of these healings. **The healing of discarnate spirits, thought forms, limiting mental concepts, mental coercion and the severing of psychic bonds can be done simply by asking,** using the tools and techniques given on page 31. We strongly recommend utilizing these tools before and during meditation if you sense any negative influences, as well as in your everyday lives. Clearing the space before you meditate allows you to expand further in consciousness, because you only expand to the level that you feel safe.

These healings can also be done for others. You are not trespassing on their free will; you are only allowing their free will to come forward without any outer influences.

Healing Negative Influences

We spoke earlier about the vibrational lifting process, and how Humanity is evolving into greater awareness and sensitivity to other planes and dimensions. In the first book, we spoke of malevolent spirits—deceased loved ones whose passing may have been traumatic, leaving a lot of unfinished business. They are often referred to as ghosts or poltergeists, which are often deceased mischievous children. We refer to them as discarnate spirits. There are also other negative influences such as thought forms, limiting mental concepts and psychic bonds of a manipulative or lower vibrational nature. These can all be healed using a few simple tools in conjunction with your main teacher and guide.

You all have an Angelic Guide or Ascended Master waiting in the wings to assist you. There is not one of you that does not have one, and some have several. It is very easy to discern the nature of a spirit and what level they are coming from. The more unconditional love and joy expressed, the more you are honored and empowered as a sovereign God with a divine right to free will and self-determination, and the more you are held accountable and responsible for your own awakening and healing process, the higher is the level.

Always trust your intuition and your feelings as to the nature and intentions of the individual, seen or unseen, that you are working with. By their fruits you shall know them. A good rule of thumb is, "Just because you are dead does not mean you are enlightened." Names, images and hierarchical orders are also unimportant, especially if you are to become dependent upon them or subject to them. The greatest of all Gods are bound by an immutable law known as free will. They can only inspire and make suggestions. To live your life for you and make all your decisions is interfering with your own evolution. There has been divine intervention in the past, yet it was only to ensure the continuation of evolution.

There are teachers and healers with various psychic abilities below what is known as the psychic barrier in the astral levels. They can help in certain ways, yet their teachings are limited, for they are not yet Christed. Rather than have someone tell you your future, why not learn to create your own destiny? You have been doing it all along. Why not do it consciously? This is what is taught by the Christed levels.

In doing these healings, call upon your own Christ self or your main teacher or guide coming from the Christ vibration. We strongly suggest using the aforementioned guidelines to discern the nature of the entity you are working with. If your intuition or feelings are telling you something isn't right, do a healing until it feels clear. Don't worry about insulting your main teacher or guide. They are very patient and understanding.

Again, **we also strongly recommend using these tools before meditation,** because you will only expand in consciousness to the level that you feel safe and clear. If you clear your space first, your space gets bigger.

These healings can be used anywhere, anyplace, even in the marketplace, to bring peace and clarity to any situation. They do not have to be blurted out, so as to become a spectacle. They can be done silently within. What you are dealing with is consciousness, and it can be healed in consciousness. Speaking the healings is best done in private or within groups of like-minded people.

The entities you are healing exist in a mental realm. Whatever you speak or hold within the mind manifests on their level of experience. When you tell them they are filled and surrounded with the Christ light and the Christ love, it happens instantaneously. **When you ask your main teacher and guide to take them to their perfect place, they appear to them in a mental body, and it is done.**

A Christed Master can appear in many places at once. That is what omnipresence is all about, so do not think you are taking up too much of their time, taking them away from a more important task. They can be very personal with you and many others, all at the same time. Besides, they are not bound by time, and can go forward or backward, which is a potential within you also.

Do the healings with conviction. If it does not feel clear, continue to do the healings, because there may be more than one entity in need of a healing, which is more often the case.

I and a host are with you. The very Source itself is within you, waiting for the call to come forward. Know that you are not alone and that you are greatly loved, cherished and worthy of this work. We will not leave you in worship. We are here to take you all the way home into your own self-mastery.

Tools and Techniques for Healing Negative Influences

1. Close your aura by visualizing white or gold light around your body.

2. Call upon your chosen cultural representative of God, be it Jesus, Buddha, Baba ji, Mary, Mohammed, White Eagle or another one of the Beautiful Many Christed Ones.

3. Tell any unwanted entities they are healed and forgiven, lifted and enlightened. Repeat this if you feel there are several.

4. Tell them they are filled and surrounded by the Christ light and the Christ love.

5. Ask your chosen representative to take them to their perfect place.

6. Ask that all negative thought forms and limiting mental concepts be dissolved and lifted in the light of truth.

7. Ask that all psychic bonds be severed and that the auras of all concerned be closed to all but spirit of the highest vibration.

It is also wise to ask that any residual energies be cleansed from your own fields, and end each session with a love or power feeding from Spirit to energize yourself or the group with which you may be working. These simple tools will empower you and take you safely into other planes, dimensions and expansions in consciousness.

There is a shadow side. **Always know you are divinely protected and that you are in good company.** Know that you have a divine right to free will and self-determination, and that your mind and your body are yours and yours alone, and all will be well.

Unique, Yet One

This next understanding concerns your identity. Many fear expansion and experiencing higher levels of consciousness, because they believe they will lose their identity.

Identity is honored on all levels. You will always keep your identity. All that you will lose is a lot of excess baggage. **There are many things you have falsely identified with,** such as the lower vibrational attitudes and emotions, the wounds, traumas and wrong conclusions from past experiences.

The past experiences are what make you the unique individual that you are. When you heal and release the past, you will not lose the wisdom gained from the experience and have to repeat the experience. The wisdom from these experiences settles within the soul. If left unresolved and the right conclusions have not been gained from the experiences, they become blocks and patterns which manifest and magnetize repeat performances of experiences such as undesirable people and events, including diseases, into your daily lives. By engaging the higher consciousness, these blocks and patterns can be dissolved gracefully, the wisdom can settle in the soul, and the perfect incarnation can come forward. You will still be the unique character you always were, minus the baggage.

So what happens after you release the baggage? You become a whole and healthy individual who can access more of the Higher Consciousness and Energy into your unique personal endeavors. You also gain access to other planes and dimensions along a vibrational continuum.

As you expand in consciousness and move what seems to be upward along this vibrational continuum, you begin to experience different aspects of yourself. You first may encounter the lower astral levels, which are not often pleasant. This is why it is wise to learn how to heal unseen negative influences and invoke protection. Then further along the way you will encounter your etheric self, the perfect incarnation often referred to as the soul. This etheric self will have a name and be living a life on the etheric level. Although everything on the etheric level is physical to your etheric self, it is non-physical to your third dimensional reality.

The same goes for your Christ self, your God self and your Cosmic self, expanding all the way back to the Source, which has no identity, yet encompasses all identity. Now that some of you are thoroughly confused as to your identity, it's time for the old wrap-around.

Many become confused when they experience their etheric self and realize it is not a separate being but themselves on another level of consciousness. They get even more confused when they meet their Christ self and it tells them, "I AM YOU." They back up and say, "Wait a minute! How can I be my personality self, my etheric self and now my Christ self?" Then along comes their God self and says, "YOU ARE MY HANDS AND FEET."

You are a multidimensional being existing on a vibrational continuum all the way back to the Source itself. That is why the Apostle Paul said we have bodies terrestrial and bodies celestial. We have a body within a body within a body, into infinity. The further you expand upon this continuum, your identity expands also, taking in other identities. **At the furthest point of identity, you are one with all life, all consciousness.** That is your true identity. You are GOD,

---

the one consciousness that encompasses all consciousness, everyone, everything and nothing. You are a focal point in a sea of consciousness that can expand from a singular identity to the one consciousness that encompasses all consciousness. That is why it is written, "Ye are Gods." Even your personality self is a condensed version of GOD. Before you get too arrogant and smug, so is a rock.

That which resides within you is what condensed a rock from consciousness into light, then into energy, and once more into mass. That is what makes you lord over the rock, your body and all physical mass. You will never own your lordship and divine heritage if you identify only with the physical and your personality self. **The whole universe resides within you.** Go within, expand in consciousness, and become one with the one consciousness that encompasses all consciousness. That is your true identity.

> *The whole universe resides within you.*

In doing this, I might add, you must let go of all fear, unworthiness and the graven images of man. This includes doctrines, false beliefs and limiting mental concepts, all of which have created GOD as an image separate from man, Nature and life. **Your image of GOD must include all life, which also includes you.** Any other image is limited, far from omnipresence, and created not to empower you but to enslave you. Your true identity is a loving, joyous, wise and powerful manifesting God.

Now that we have addressed the "Who am I?" let us now address the second question asked by those on the path to self-discovery: "Why am I here?" **You are a God, born of the original light from which nothing has been withheld, who has chosen to condense and lower itself down through the dimensions into a personality, occupy a body and have an adventure.** It is an adventure into the apex of creation, the physical, which is the last density of GOD.

If you did not experience the flesh, free will and powerful emotions (necessary attributes of the Christ Consciousness), you would be incomplete. It takes mastery of all levels, all planes and all dimensions to become a Christ. This includes mastery of free will and powerful emotions. That is how you manifest.

Creation begins in consciousness by using the will, embracing the thought emotionally and calling it into form. You have been doing it, some consciously and most unconsciously, all along. **You are here to gain the wisdom from the manifestations and further your development through experience.** You are manifesting and magnetizing people and events into your daily lives in order to gain wisdom, the grandest treasure of all.

You are not a human seeking a spiritual experience; you are GOD seeking a human experience. You have already done spirit repeatedly. Welcome to the greatest and most challenging adventure of all, and that is mastering the apex of creation, which is the physical, free will and powerful emotions.

The greatest school of self-mastery ever created is an emerald planet known as Earth, a planet where eventually all will, through experience, choose love to be the manifesting force behind all creation. You have manifested and magnetized a lot of people and events into your daily lives for the experience.

You have never made a mistake. Before the experience you were innocent. Now that you have experienced what you don't want, gain the wisdom from the experience. Allow it to settle in the soul as wisdom, release it and go forward. The only mistake you have made is to judge, condemning yourself, accepting the judgments of others and allowing guilt to hold you in the past.

You are refining and exacting what you do want. How would you know what you want unless you experience a lot of little "don't wants" to measure by? If the "don't wants" keep manifesting, you have not yet gained the wisdom from the experience. Forgive yourself for magnetizing and manifesting the people and the events that led to the experience. Now that you know what you don't want, let it go. It is that simple. The only reason it will return is because you have not gained the wisdom from it, haven't released it and allowed it to settle within the soul. That is why you are here, to gain the wisdom from experience.

The Earth is merely an action/reaction world known as the plane of demonstration where consciousness creates reality. It is a place where eternal Gods come to gain wisdom from experience and master powerful emotions, free will and have an adventure. It is the greatest challenge of all, embarked upon by the bravest of Angels.

This next understanding is to clarify another aspect concerning identity, which is hard to comprehend on a linear level or where separation is so commonplace. **Your soul is like a hologram, where each piece holds the complete picture within it.** It is like a piece of GOD, and each piece contains the whole of GOD. Within each piece is the potential to become the whole.

There are immense beings who have the ability to divide their consciousness and take up residence within many individuals at once. They can merge their consciousness with others, giving them access to a much bigger picture, or what we call Higher Consciousness and Energy.

> *Even at the soul level, one can occupy more than one body.*

Even at the soul level, one can occupy more than one body. This is what is referred to as a walk-in, where a soul decides to leave and an oversoul or advanced soul decides to pick up where that individual left. This is not a possession, as when lower vibrational beings with unfinished business try a hostile takeover. It is done with the consent of the individual who has chosen to leave, and always for some higher purpose.

There are Christ or I AM transitions, where you merge with your Christ or I AM self. There are also initiations where you are initiated into the house of another ("house" refers to consciousness). You can be initiated into the house of Jesus, Baba ji, Mary, Buddha, Mohammed and a whole host of other enlightened Masters, even my house, the house of Cazekiel, if you so choose. There is room for everyone. You don't lose your personality or identity in doing so; you just gain access to more unconditional love, joy, wisdom and peace, a more expanded state of awareness. Your sense of identity expands into oneness, while still retaining your uniqueness.

Soon you will find out your personality self and your body are rather petty when it comes to the big picture. Your body and your personality are important; and rather than discard them or judge them to be less than holy, bring them into alignment with your soul, its purpose and the higher bodies.

Love your bodies, take care of them. Love your personalities. Only you can be you, and your uniqueness expands creation. GOD chose to become you, to inhabit a body and have the adventure of the personality.

There is soul personality, or soul ego, which is free of the misperceptions, wounds, traumas and wrong conclusions from past experiences found within the alter ego of the personality formed in your present Earth sojourn. **When we say, "Bring your personality and your body into alignment with your soul purpose," it is there where the blueprint for the perfect incarnation resides—your true purpose for being.**

Relax your grip on your identity. Loosen up and lighten up. Expand into other houses, and glean all they have to offer, that which they share so freely.

Stop being so linear and factual. After all, most of the facts you base your identity on are erroneous anyway. If people are telling you that you are acting bizarre and spacey, tell them you are acting more unlimited. There is more joy in it. Isn't that what you are after, more joy?

Sovereign Love

There is a love that transcends all love. It is sovereign, unconditional and eternal. It is not dependent upon the love, acceptance or approval of others. It does not judge, condemn, compete or war upon another. It does not have to defend its truth; it owns it. It allows. It is an all-powerful, immutable force which can never be conquered or destroyed. It is and always will be. It is a force which, when called upon, will move mountains, create miracles, lift and empower all who call upon it to meet any challenge.

There is one thing, however, it cannot do. Love cannot trespass on the will of another or work in a fashion that is not highest and best for all concerned. It can remove the clouds to help all concerned see better. It can heal and remove negative influences. It can guide and protect when called upon. It is an all-knowing force that is aware of the highest and best good for everyone and sees the purposeful good in everything. It is a great amplifier of the highest vibration, which causes a quickening of that which is out of alignment or of a lower vibration.

If you surrender to love, then it will lift and empower you, often healing you gracefully. If you resist it or choose not to align with or allow love to be the manifesting force behind all creation, it amplifies that resistance and brings forth the physical manifestation that corresponds with the misalignment. It accelerates the reaction to every action and the manifestation of all attitudes and emotions. It does not do it to punish. It does not possess an ego to judge a good thought from a bad thought. It loves everything into being. **Love's favorite words are, "AS YOU WISH," knowing that with every experience, every manifestation, comes wisdom.** It knows you are eternal. Even if you choose death to gain wisdom, it allows. It is lawless.

The plane of demonstration known as Earth, however, has laws. The greatest of all laws is the Law of Love. **The**

understanding that consciousness creates reality and love must be the manifesting force behind all creation. The action/reaction principle and the power of forgiveness, non-judgment and grace are all relative to understanding and aligning oneself with the ultimate power in the universe.

Within each and every individual is a great God, born of the original light. It is eternal, it has a name, and it is the working duplicate of the original light from which nothing was withheld. It is pure, unconditional love and joy; "Bliss." **It operates as sovereign love and has all of the qualities of sovereign love.** It is bound by the same principles and honors an immutable law known as

> *Within each and every individual is a great God, born of the original light.*

free will. It always manifests what is in the highest and best good for all concerned. It sees the purposeful good in everything, and it will bring things to you and take things away in your highest and best good. When you consciously engage it, the power increases a hundred-fold. **When you are in alignment and a clear channel for love, it increases a million-fold.**

When evoking this power, there are a few understandings which come with engaging the light. When engaging the light, the intentions must be pure. It must always be used for the highest and best good for all concerned, and never to control or manipulate.

If you are not a clear vessel or channel for consciousness and energy, the blocks and patterns within self will also be amplified and accelerated. They can be healed gracefully, depending on the resistance or the ability to surrender and release. **For those of you who decide it is too much trouble, too painful, to awaken and heal, or you would rather be doing something else, we have a little news flash: IT IS NO LONGER AN OPTION WITHIN THIS UNIVERSE.**

Sovereign love is coming. It is the love of GOD. Higher Consciousness and Energy is amplifying and accelerating the consciousness upon this plane which determines the realities individually and collectively you choose to experience. It is not judging you or condemning you. It is exalting, embracing and manifesting everything.

There is a quickening in the lag time between the action and the reaction. As you sow, so shall you reap, yet the time between the sowing and the reaping will become almost instantaneous. As you believe, so it is, yet the beliefs will manifest much sooner. **Those who choose love to be the manifesting force behind every thought, every deed and all creation, will be exalted.** Those who choose to change their beliefs will change the world. That is destiny.

Where is GOD throughout all the dramas? GOD is unconditionally loving them into existence, saying, "AS YOU WISH."

Come to me with an open mind and a loving heart, and I will fill them with wisdom and love. Come to me with fear, doubt, anger and skepticism, and of that too you shall have your fill. I AM a Divine mirror and amplifier of that which is within self. What you seek is what you will find. It will be as you wish.

Cazekiel

Chakras and Subtle Bodies, Centers of Consciousness

We begin with the main emphasis on the first three chakras, which are where the majority of Humanity are focused. The first three are also where most of the healing is necessary. These chakras respond to transmissions of light, sound and consciousness.

As we move up the chakra system, beginning with the first, located at the base of the spine, we find the color red. The second chakra is orange, the third is yellow, the fourth is green, the fifth is light blue, the sixth is indigo or often seen as white, and the seventh is violet. The chakra system corresponds with the colors of the rainbow.

There can be mixtures of the colors within the system and darker muddy colors, which indicate a need for healing. The auric field will also be a mixture of colors, and again, the darker muddy colors within the auric field also indicate a healing is necessary. There are those whose auric fields have a dominant color throughout, which is representative of their purpose. Each color or ray of light has a focus or a primary function.

Sound is very effective in healing the chakras of any denser energies, which are also representative of lower vibrational attitudes and emotions. There are notes and tones that correspond with each chakra. There are also notes and tones and colors that correspond with the organs and glands within the body. We will give you a chart representing the colors, notes and tones, which will help you understand and heal the body on all levels [see next page].

Consciousness is the greatest healer of all, for everything begins in consciousness. In the beginning was the word, yet the thought precedes the word, and light precedes sound. The energies that coagulate to create the body are first born in consciousness. In other words, **your body is nothing more than coagulated thought. The dark or muddy colors within the chakras and auric field are lower vibrational attitudes and emotions blocking the perfect incarnation often referred to as THE IDEAL. Prayer, meditation and color or sound therapy can all help heal the body**.

We will give you understandings, tools and techniques to help you heal and balance these energy systems. At first when you start using these techniques you may not feel anything. You may even feel a bit foolish. As you become more vibrant, healthy and more sensitive, the feelings will become stronger,

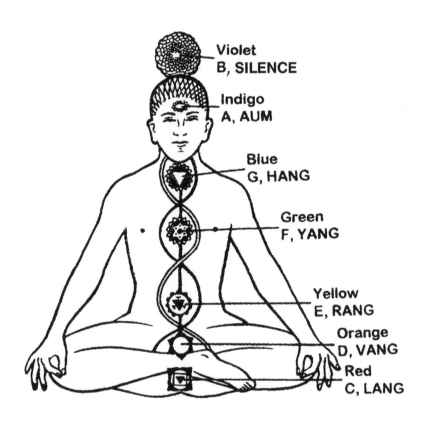

Violet
B, SILENCE

Indigo
A, AUM

Blue
G, HANG

Green
F, YANG

Yellow
E, RANG

Orange
D, VANG

Red
C, LANG

The color, musical note and sound
associated with each of the seven chakras.

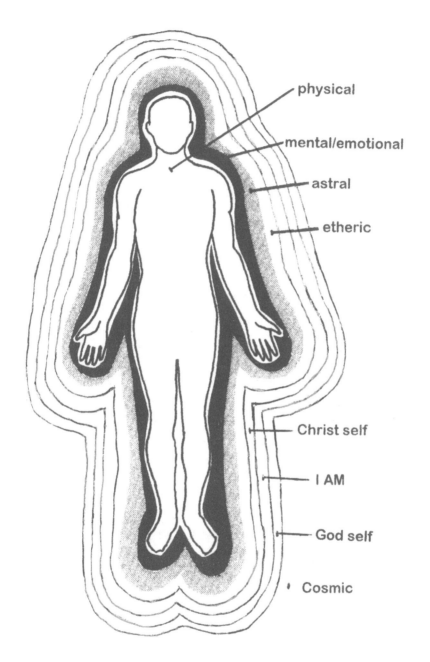

physical

mental/emotional

astral

etheric

Christ self

I AM

God self

Cosmic

The layers of the human body, the subtle bodies.

and you will recognize the value in using these techniques.

There will be incredible advances and developments in the transmissions of color, sound and powerful consciousness utilized as therapies, as Humanity continues to evolve. As the new Higher Consciousness and Energy continues to inspire new developments in these fields, and the physical body is lifted into more of an energy body, the body in the future will be treated more as a system of energy, sound, light and consciousness.

There is a matrix of consciousness and energy, a body within a body, existing as a more expanded state of awareness. These bodies within bodies expand infinitely and are known as the subtle bodies.

The auric fields and subtle bodies can already be photographed and measured. The energies within the chakra system can be measured, and the effects of the transmissions of sound, light and powerful healing consciousness can also be measured. There are already devices which can heal and bring balance to the body. It can all be done through consciousness, and the devices prove the existence of the auric field, the subtle bodies, the chakras, and the effects that light, sound and consciousness have upon them.

Scientists, through such devices, are making real what has been known by ancient mystics throughout the East and the West for thousands of years. We will continue to inspire both physical and nonphysical use and exploration of these therapies directed for the betterment of mankind. This too is a by-product of the Higher Consciousness and Energy pressing hard upon this plane of which we are a part.

Chakra Clearing Meditation

1. Begin by sitting comfortably in a chair or on the floor. Visualize yourself and the room filled with light. Close your aura to all but Spirit and see yourself surrounded by the white light of the Christ vibration.

2. Call upon your representative of the Father to assist you, or ask the Father to assist you.

3. Visualize a white or golden light spinning and swirling at the crown of your head.

4. Move this light down to your third eye (located on your forehead, just above and between your eyes). Spin and swirl the light through this area. Visualize it clearing this chakra.

5. Move it downward to the throat chakra, repeating the process.

6. Move it downward to the next chakra (the heart), again spinning and swirling the light.

7. Move it downward to the solar plexus; spinning, swirling and clearing.

8. Then downward to the area just below the navel.

9. Finally, move it to the root chakra, the base of the spine.

10. Now take this light energy and create an anchor into the Earth. This will help ground you.

11. Now, visualize a crystalline tube that is impenetrable. Visualize this tube rising from you and attaching to the Godhead. Feel it click into place. Know that nothing can enter this tube but Spirit of the highest vibration.

12. Run the golden ball from the base of your spine upwards to the Godhead.

13. Now, feel the pure love and joy of spirit descending into your body, filling you with Grace.

14. You have created a clear path of golden energy upon which Spirit can travel.

Practice this daily and soon you will be a clear receiver for Spirit in all that you say and do. If you would like to focus on just one chakra, then visualize energy of the color associated with that chakra and spin and swirl it in the chakra. Many have received miraculous healings, powerful love feedings and vibrational liftings using this exercise.

Survival, Sex and Power

Survival, sex and power concern the first three chakras of the human chakra energy system. The new Higher Consciousness and Energies play an important part concerning these three chakras.

There is another understanding concerning the nature of mind or consciousness, which is not limited to the brain. **The brain is just a receiver that attunes to consciousness.** There are many subtle bodies which also store consciousness that exist beyond the physical, and the chakras are channels of this consciousness and energy. Each chakra categorizes the consciousness and energy.

The first chakra concerns base survival issues. The second concerns sexual and creative energies, and the third concerns power. For centuries these three chakras have been misunderstood, misaligned and to this day are being frequently abused. **Love felt, which is the fourth chakra, along with love spoken (the fifth), GOD seen in all things (the sixth), and I AM GOD (the seventh), are invading the first three chakras, healing them and bringing them back into alignment.** This is a manifestation of the vibrational lifting and healing process.

All of the unresolved issues, unhealed wounds, traumas and wrong conclusions from past experiences are surfacing concerning these three chakras. They are being healed and realigned, and the abuse of these energies will no longer be appropriate. In other words, people are waking up and becoming empowered, and the misalignments and abuses of these energies will not only be obvious, it will not be tolerated.

These energies often combine in unhealthy combinations and create dramas within one's personal relationships and life, which result in negative experiences. Take survival issues: **If one has a fear of survival, he or she may use sex and power inappropriately to ensure his or her survival.** There are those who, due to fear and a low self-esteem, arrogantly use their power and sexual energies to control and manipulate others.

There are those who equate money and position with self-worth and power, and use money or their position to control and manipulate others, preying upon their fears, insecurities or base survival issues. They rely heavily upon their outer appearances, and their gifts have hooks—the bigger the gift, the bigger the hook. Those who bite the hook, accepting these gifts, often lose their freedom. They have been purchased, so to speak, and buying something implies ownership.

As we have mentioned before, those who desire to own and control others are they themselves controlled by the next move of those beneath them.

Control has many worries; unconditional love has none.

Here is something they should contemplate: **"Control has many worries; unconditional love has none."**

There are those who use their positions of power or wealth to take love, rather than make love, to bolster their egos and for sense gratification. Those who fall victim to this behavior will be exalted and empowered. A new sense of self-worth will come to the victims, causing a separation, and they will not allow it in the future.

As you can see, the abuses and misuses of these three energies are rampant upon the Earth at this time. **The ancient wounds and wrong conclusions concerning survival, the abuse or misalignment of sexual energies and the blatant abuses of power are all coming to a close.** There is a quickening, which is cyclically and exponentially bringing these abuses and misalignments forward.

The diseases which are a physical counterpart of the misuse and misalignment of these energies are surfacing everywhere. Tyrants are falling upon their own swords in their abuses of power, not only due to the diseases they call upon themselves, but by the very reaction to their actions, which is also being accelerated. These dramas are surfacing everywhere, being acted out, and if not healed, people are checking out.

Arrogance, stubbornness, blame and falling into the role of victim will not be appropriate responses in the days to come. **Now is the time to take responsibility and own your creations. It is up to each individual to break the chain of experiences.** No one is going to save you or break your chains, for the one you believe is going to save you becomes but another link in the chain. **The savior, victim and persecutor dramas are coming to a close. They will be accelerated until you have had enough.**

Surrender your wounds, traumas and wrong conclusions to your own God self. Have the humbleness and humility to allow the wisdom to settle in the soul, thus relieving you from recreating the experience. Find a process-oriented technique that works for you, one that is not limited to this life only. The body will heal itself once the pattern is removed, the clouds will disappear, and you will see clearly the reason for the experience. There is purposeful good in everything.

There are bands or waves of energy passing through the Earth which carry with them consciousness. These bands of energy are best understood as lessons for the collective consciousness. **As each band passes through, there is a group lesson concerning the issue that band was sent to address. If there are unhealed or unresolved memories concerning the issue or lesson contained in the band of consciousness and energy, it is amplified and brought to the surface.**

If you were to have a group gather during the peak of

one of these bands of consciousness and energy and ask each individual to write in one word what he or she is feeling or processing, you would be amazed at how many would have the same issue. These bands of consciousness and energy build in intensity, have peaks, and are then followed by integration periods. They are cyclic, and increase exponentially.

Often these bands of energy correspond with the chakras and the consciousness within them. The consciousness and energy sent within the band will be the ideal, and it will call forward any abuses or misalignments which do not match that ideal.

Uniqueness is still honored. We are not all turning into clones. We are only healing the wounds, traumas and wrong conclusions concerning that particular lesson. For example, let us say the consciousness and energy band concerning survival, which corresponds with the first chakra, is beginning to peak. The fear of survival and all the wrong conclusions from past experiences, including ancient struggles for survival, will be amplified, and will surface to be processed and healed, so as to settle in the soul as wisdom.

> *Uniqueness is still honored.*

The second band of energy is released, and it amplifies the second chakra, which is sexual and creative energy. Any abuses and misalignments are again amplified, and also surface to be processed and healed.

Then the third band is released, which corresponds with the third chakra, which is power. All the abuses and misalignments concerning power which do not correspond with self-empowerment and love, which always empowers others, begin to surface.

The unhealed wounds, traumas and wrong conclusions from past experiences, as well as the abuses and misalignments of these energies in all three chakras, can be intermingled and play upon each other. Let us say fear of survival has surfaced and has been denied or ignored, sexual abuses or misalignments are amplified, and then comes the power band corresponding with the third chakra. A woman who, due to fear of survival, misuses her sexual and power chakras in a controlling, manipulative way for security will create a drama to mirror back to her the unhealed or unresolved issues. Even if there is no basis in reality, she will project her beast upon her lover. If she is stubborn and refuses to own her issues, she will recreate the same drama again and again with more intensity, or a disease which corresponds with the unresolved attitude or emotion. This disease will correspond with the area of the body or chakra in which that particular attitude or emotion expresses.

If a man has survival down and is very secure, yet misuses sexual and power energies to control or dominate, he will also have multiple undesirable dramas, and eventually a disease, if he continues in denial. The disease will also correspond with the area of the body or the chakra in which that particular attitude and emotion expresses.

We are addressing the first three chakras because this is where the majority of the healing work is happening. Survival, sex and power are the three most misaligned and imbalanced energies on the planet. It doesn't take a genius to know when the power band is coming through. One only has to watch the news to see the tyrants come forward, only to fall from the reactions to their actions. Because of the quickening, what used to take months and years is occurring in days and weeks.

The fourth band of consciousness and energy is love, unconditional love. As this band flows through, old wounds of the heart begin to surface, and lost lovers come back to haunt you. The wisdom is also there to draw upon, so as to heal and release the past.

Love is invading the three lower chakras as well, and where love is not the manifesting force behind creation, there will be discomfort. The discomfort will be mental, emotional or physical, depending on your ability to change, release and heal.

The Next Four Bands

The next four bands of consciousness and energy correspond with the next four chakras. Love felt for all things is the fourth, love expressed is the fifth, GOD seen in all things is the sixth, and I AM GOD is the seventh. The seven chakras are also known as seals.

We spoke earlier about the fourth band, which is love felt for all things. As this band of consciousness and energy passes through, it amplifies and accelerates the wounds, traumas and wrong conclusions from past experiences concerning love felt.

If one has not felt loved in past relationships, which includes family, friends and lovers, these feelings will surface. The abandonment or loss of mothers, fathers, family members, friends and lovers, or them not being there emotionally, falls under this category. As these are processed and healed, a warm feeling and love for all things begins to take place. This is the energy that will be prevalent on the Earth after the vibrational lifting and healing process moves further into completion.

The fifth band is love expressed. We often say things which are unloving and nonsupportive, and judge and condemn others for not conforming to our picture of reality. This is an abuse or misuse of the fifth chakra.

The word has power. When you are speaking the word, you are creating a reality. This reality can be projected upon another, and he or she will feel or act out that reality. The power of your word often corresponds with the power of your consciousness, and the subjectivity of the one you are speaking to will also determine whether he or she shields from it or acts it out.

Thoughts are things waiting to manifest, and it is through the word that they come into manifestation. Scary? It is. Can you imagine the abuse and misuse of the word in today's society? **Fortunately, those who most often**

misuse the word are connected into social consciousness, which has very little manifesting power behind it; nonetheless, they are very slowly creating undesirable events in their future.

By using the word consciously to manifest positive and loving realities, we are tapping into a greater power and can dissolve and undo these undesirable events. **Prayer is a form of using the word to dissolve the miscreations before they manifest, or to change a situation that is undesirable.** The more powerful the consciousness, the quicker the prayer is realized.

If the prayer does not manifest, there can be many reasons. One, there is a block or unresolved issue in your own consciousness; two, it is not in your highest and best good, and something better is on the horizon; or three, it was not in the highest and best good for the one you were praying for, or they could not accept the gift.

I must caution you when praying for another. Always pray for the highest and best good for all concerned, without manipulation. Do not pray that someone behave differently according to your picture of reality, or pray that they return to you. That is not honoring free will, and it may be in their highest and best good to leave and create a space for something else. This takes discipline.

Your words and prayers are very powerful. Consciousness creates reality through the word. Remember, love expressed is what the fifth chakra is designed for; expressing otherwise will create undesirable events, or even disease within the throat area.

The sixth band of energy is GOD seen in all things. This is associated with clairvoyance. We can use this gift in many ways. When the sixth chakra is open, you can see other planes and dimensions. This often includes thought forms and discarnate spirits within the astral level. They can be healed very easily using the tools on page 31.

This also includes seeing the Beautiful Many Saints, Sages and Ascended Masters who are divinely intervening on Humanity's behalf, and opens you up to the other dimensional beings who are helping Humanity. As we have mentioned before, it also brings to awareness great interdimensional ships that are just out of range of the five senses, which is becoming very commonplace in today's society. You know—those dreams and visions, those phantoms you see out of the corners of your eyes that vanish because you turn to look at them. These are all by-products of the sixth chakra opening, due to the sixth band of energy.

The seventh band of energy has the highest consciousness and energy within it: I AM GOD. Did you know there is a whole host of beings mythologically known as Archangels that exist on the seventh level of understanding? They have come to realize that there is no separation in omnipresence. They are one with GOD, and possess all of the love, joy, power and wisdom of the Source of all that is.

Did you know that you, too, possess that capability, and they were once just like you? **This is known as the seventh seal, and when it opens, the gates of heaven open along with it. It is hard to imagine a world of seventh level beings, yet one day you will see that world.** It is coming to this world, and is the greater part of the consciousness and energy that is divinely intervening on behalf of Humanity.

Sacred Relationships

As the vibrational lifting and healing process continues, there will be a forward movement into sacred relationships. The fears, wounds and traumas of the past will all come forward in every arena to be healed.

Relationships are not limited to friends, families and lovers. There are business relationships, relationships between countries, the governments of those countries, and their people. Their collective fears, wounds and traumas will also surface, along with the reactions to their actions.

There is individual karma and collective karma. The

lessons, the right conclusions from past experiences, as well as right action, will come forward. There is also the relationship to life and the platform for life, Earth, which is sacred. Those who have a sacred relationship with GOD, Humanity and Nature are truly blessed and will fare well in the days to come.

Before a sacred relationship can occur in any one of these given areas, the reactions and all that which is unbalanced or unresolved must come forward. Thus the vibrational lifting is being orchestrated by those who hold all life as sacred.

The most adventurous relationship of all during this process is the relationship between man and woman. We have spoken earlier about the first three chakras, which represent survival, sex and power. This is where the greatest healings are occurring at this time.

When you move into the fourth chakra, you move into love, and **love always empowers, never overpowers. That is when the relationship becomes sacred.** It is when the power struggles and manipulations end, and soul purpose begins. Although the first three chakras are still active, they are not driven by fear or the wounds and traumas of the past. They come into alignment with love, and love is expressed through each chakra. In order for this to occur, both individuals must be sovereign in their own identity, aligned with their own unique purpose, love and accept themselves and walk in their own power.

Love always empowers, never overpowers.

There are no dependencies in sacred relationships. It is a coming together, each bringing his or her own unique talents and abilities in a combination that complements the other. The combination of the two becomes greater than apart, and rather than a constriction or competition, there is a sharing, along with more freedom and a stronger base from which to operate. As long as there is equality and love, there will be abundance on every level.

There are many who have taken the independence thing too far. They believe they must be single to maintain their power. **It is possible to maintain one's independence and be in a relationship at the same time.** It is a dance where each comes together in shared purpose and desire and moves apart in unique purpose and desire. The freedom to do this is when the jealousies and dependencies end, and the unconditional love and trust begin.

Trust is another factor that is earned over time, and without it there is little foundation to build upon. **Trust is not a binding commitment that diminishes freedom. It is a matter of integrity, noble virtue, honor, shared purpose and holding one's relationship sacred.** It is not a contract or a doctrine that creates this. It is a soul quality, and unions of the soul do not need the false security of a contract or a doctrine.

Those commitments which are binding and where freedom is diminished will go through endless power struggles in the future. Those based upon dependencies and those which are based upon survival, sex and power without a higher purpose will also see hard times. Those commitments made by the ego in alignment with social consciousness are going to experience turmoil when the soul consciousness and purpose begin to emerge.

Soul purpose is often in complete contradiction with one's present status. It is a by-product of enlightenment. There is a saying, **"There are no perfect men or women in the world, only perfect intentions."** When we make agreements, we do so with the most honorable intentions, yet no one knows what the future holds or the plans of Spirit, which is often called the Great Mystery.

We make decisions and commitments according to our beliefs at the time. **When we align with our soul and its purpose, our beliefs often change, as well as our direction.** A war ensues, and it is a war between the soul and the personality or ego.

In many cases, when the soul emerges, it finds itself greatly constricted by choices made in the past and the box created by the personality. Desires change, directions change, and we begin to see with new eyes. What once served us in the past and was comfortable often becomes very uncomfortable and a detriment to our soul's purpose and evolution. We know we must go forward and evolve, yet that means change, the unknown, and an end to our comfort zones.

The soul will continuously press hard to come forth, and will not be denied its purpose. Try as one will, if the relationship is not in alignment with one's highest and best good, it will end. There is purposeful good even in this, because both will be free to expand into a greater love and break the chains that diminish their joy. The sooner they release the past and open to a future of limitless possibilities, the better.

A sacred relationship in its most unlimited form is a seven-chakra union. It is a union where I AM GOD (the seventh), and GOD seen in all things (the sixth), love expressed (the fifth), and love felt for all things (the fourth), all come together in balance and harmony with the first three chakras. *Very few have the love, steadfastness and courage to enter a seven-chakra union or relationship. It would be like embracing an Angel, and very few could even look upon one. Imagine everything coming up at once—the fears, wounds, traumas and the projections.*

There are even those who, despite the appearance before them, would be so damn sure it was the Angel's stuff not theirs. If an Angel opened the gates to heaven and said, "Come walk with me and be my beloved mate," many would find every way possible to sabotage the affair, rather than look at their own fears, unworthiness and mistrust.

You wonder why the enlightened ones reside high in the mountains or in Nature or why the Angelic Guides and Ascended Masters, as well as other spiritually advanced beings, do not walk among you? You are very fickle, and in some cases very dangerous. It is very uncomfortable to be among the lower vibrational attitudes, emotions and energies. This is why they are engaging you a little at a time in subtle ways, and can only lift the vibration of Humanity and the Earth very slowly. **So before you meet your Angelic mate, there will be a lot of junior Angels coming your way as divine mirrors to reflect back to you what you both need to heal.** Like attracts like.

The healing process is cyclic and exponentially increasing, which is creating a lot of turmoil and confusion, followed by periods of integration. It is like a boil that must first fester before the final eruption, and after that the healing comes. Nonetheless, there are a lot of mini-eruptions going on in all levels, as well as full blown explosions in others. The hurricanes, storms, earthquakes and volcanoes are Nature's reflections of that which is happening on the mental and emotional levels of the collective. That is where a stormy relationship got its name, and relationships are becoming as a collective very stormy and explosive.

So how does one survive the slings and arrows of stormy relationships? By loving self, becoming sovereign and owning that which you are feeling and the people and events you magnetized to you according to your consciousness. Projecting and blaming only disempowers the individual and puts the power outside of self. It begins the victim, savior, persecutor triangle all over again, which is a whole book in itself.

As said before, the only reason anyone has any power over you is because you want something from them, *and that something, whether it be love, joy, acceptance, approval or security, can be manifested by the loving, joyous, wise and powerful manifesting God within YOU.* When you become the victim, which is not a very pretty sight

> *The only reason anyone has any power over you is because you want something from them.*

from our perspective, what we see is a forgotten God wallowing in his own self-created misery. What was once the full flame of the original light has now become a mere spark without the knowledge of how to expand once again into the full flame. The spark feels it is undeserving of love, joy and abundance. You deserve to love and to be loved, to empower and to be empowered, to support and to be supportive, to cooperate and to have cooperation, to give and to receive all in balance.

Even the Creator desires companionship, love and that you be happy. That was the motivating force behind creation. It is not a need; it is a desire. The love of GOD does not depend upon the acceptance or approval of others, and what is given freely and unconditionally is given to all in full measure.

> *Even the Creator desires companionship.*

How much love, joy and happiness can you accept? How much are you willing to share? Do you have the courage to heal and take responsibility for the life you have created up to now? Without denial? How about all those walls you have built? Can you tear them down and trust one more time? It's up to you. A door always locks from the inside, and only you can unlock it. This will all measure the sacredness of your relationship and the heights or depths it will reach.

Moving into a more loving, joyous, unlimited life is what is waiting, as well as the embrace of your own God self. *What happens when you embrace your own God self? You often magnetize to yourself another who has also embraced his or her God self, and repel those who haven't.*

In order to have a sacred relationship, the parties concerned must hold each other, themselves and the relationship sacred. There must be a commitment driven by the soul, not the ego, and all parties must do their share to maintain the sacredness of the union. Each must have a healthy image of what a sacred relationship is, find agreement, and also have the reference points necessary for a quality relationship. There must be growth on all levels, and support in that growth.

If your image of a man is to work hard, bring home the bacon, plop down in front of the TV with a beer and mow the lawn and wash the car every weekend, I assure you the fires of passion are going to die an early death. If your image of a woman is to be in subjection to a man, clean house, buy the groceries, feed the kids and sit around watching soap operas, again the romance is destined for failure.

If you allow friends and family to control your life, and base your life on their opinions, you are going to have your own soap opera. If you allow material acquisitions, finances and keeping up with the Joneses to become first priority, forgetting about quality time together, an emptiness will set in.

If you start taking each other for granted and your eyes begin to wander, or if you begin splitting your energies by stringing along those of the opposite sex for a safety net or to compensate because of an insecurity, again the relationship is being compromised. If you do not take responsibility for the lack of love and joy in your own life, and hold others responsible, you are again setting yourself up for failure. Even failure is not a bad thing, as long as you gain the wisdom from the experience.

There are very few images of sacred man and sacred woman. There are even fewer unions of the two. What we have as reference points are in most cases unhealthy. The images passed down by our parents are often dysfunctional.

We all think we know what a sacred man, sacred woman and a sacred union are and desire it, yet there is always that wounded little boy or girl who gets in the way. There is the subconscious desire to recreate the father or mother in the relationship, even though bonding with someone who is like one's parents is also very dysfunctional. No matter how hard one tries to avoid it, the person one chooses always ends up to be one's mother or father in the end. You know— those love/hate relationships!

In order to have a healthy relationship, we first need a healthy reference point, and to address the inner child's desire to draw to it dysfunctional people, which it equates with security. **We must heal self, our inner world, before addressing the outer world, yet very few will take the inward approach.** It's always them: They did it; they screwed up; I had nothing to do with it. Regardless of that, it follows the little Universal Principle that like attracts like, or consciousness creates reality and the mirror standing in front of them. We must take full responsibility for the people and events we draw to us, gain the wisdom from the experience, forgive and release.

What are healthy male and female images? An enlightened male is balanced in his masculine and his feminine energies. He knows when to be objective and when to be subjective, leaning a little more towards the objective. He knows when to listen, when to speak, when to go within for guidance and when to act. He is balanced in his energies, and because of his physical expression will most often be more of a doer than a listener, a thinker rather than a feeler, and quick to act unless he gets too caught up in indecision.

An enlightened female is also balanced in her energies. She knows when to be objective and when to be subjective, and may lean a little more towards the subjective feeling nature and be a little more nurturing. She often will be a better listener, desire closer interaction and be more expressive emotionally.

What we are saying is, in general by nature, men and women are different, and by honoring the differences and allowing them to complement each other, the union is stronger than its separate parts. In order to create, the polarities are necessary, and both are equal. **The most desired men are those who are sensitive, know how to listen, when to act and when to allow. The most desired women are those who are loving, nurturing and assertive in their own purpose and their own truth.** The more balanced each becomes and the greater the equality, the better the union.

This next understanding is concerning the imbalances and abuse of power due to fear and the need to control. We spoke earlier about the objective/subjective or masculine/feminine balance. In order to engage the Highest Consciousness and Energy, there must be balance. It is a balanced energy. It is said that **the mind you use determines the mind in which you connect. Again, like attracts like.**

> *The mind you use determines the mind in which you connect.*

Those who engage in calling on Higher Consciousness and Energy and who are unbalanced draw to themselves unbalanced energy. They also draw to themselves unbalanced spirits who can be very controlling and manipulating, due to their own unresolved issues and imbalances.

There are many groups which in error are polarized or unbalanced, and rather than heal the imbalances, they support each other's imbalances. They desire power to compensate for the times they lost their power and were not treated equally or were victimized. The greatest of all tyrants have always been the greatest of all victims. They were driven by fear to gain power, not to empower, but to control and overpower others. They could not move out of the third chakra and evolve into the fourth, and many are there to this day.

Women, especially throughout history, have experienced tremendous abuse upon this plane. They have been traded like cattle; the spoils of war were the gold and the women. They were sold into slavery and sexually abused at a very young age, and when their youth and beauty began to fade, they were tossed out for a younger woman. They often had no say whatsoever in their destiny and were dutiful servants. According to some religions, they were soulless, had no rights and were to beware of, for they would tempt the hearts of honest men. In some countries to this day, they still must walk behind a man in servitude.

So what happens when power comes to the first three chakras and amplifies and accelerates all the unresolved issues concerning survival, sex and power? How about the cellular memory being released into the auric field and felt by the soul? Before a sacred relationship can occur, this all must come forward to be healed—it is right on schedule, and relationships will become very volatile between men and women.

Men have their issues as well. Although most men understand power, mainly because they have been at it for eons, they do not understand love as a collective. They have been forced to go on long marches, war, compete and be the protectors and providers. To show any emotions or sensitivity was seen as a weakness. It often meant the difference between losing their lives, their kingdoms and all that was dear to them. Their very survival depended upon it.

Men have to overcome centuries of not being able to express their true feelings, and tearing down those walls takes more courage than taking on an entire army single-handed. Many would gladly face the army, given the option between that and their own inner child, or the wounds and traumas of the past. They haven't been able to emotionally embrace and release their fears, sorrows and the wounds and traumas from past experiences. They are bottled up inside.

So what happens when the quickening comes to them, and all those bottled up emotions begin to surface? If they don't express or release them, they are going to explode in emotional outbursts, or the constriction will implode as a physical disease. You know—all those heart attacks and high blood pressures!

The flood gates are going to open in both men and women. Rather than warring on each other, a more equitable approach is to support each other, knowing that the process is necessary.

Be very clear before making any decisions concerning ending a relationship, as to whether it is in your highest and best good and whether or not you can further evolve in your present circumstances. Take it deep within and feel the answer. Ask yourself whether or not it is your soul's purpose to remain in the relationship, and if the commitment you made presently serves your greater good.

How does one do this? Remember that Love, the ultimate power in the universe, always empowers, never overpowers. The greatest is unconditional love, which forgives and allows. Surrender! Not to the opposite sex or another, surrender to the God within you. Call the spirit within to come forward and heal the wounds, traumas and wrong conclusions from past experiences.

If you need help, find a process-oriented therapy or someone who is balanced with whom to talk. Learn to cry, and don't stop the emotions and the feelings from flowing. Ask your own God self to lift you into love and joy, which is the truth of your being. Ask for guidance in alignment with soul purpose, courage, strength and steadfastness to follow through with your own unique purpose, despite the whole of the world.

In gatherings, always focus on unity and a coming together in the highest and best good of all, honoring unique purpose, not separation or opposition. There are extremes to avoid that dishonor the opposite sex, and engage in separation or men and women bashing.

There are a lot of wounded men and women gathering in support groups which support the imbalances. This is not so if the individuals within the groups are balanced or have the intent of healing and finding balance. Unfortunately, in many cases, this is not the intent. The energy often becomes controlling or manipulative, because power is what is sought, motivated by fear or wounds and traumas of the past.

Again, the unbalanced energy of the group and its leader draw other unbalanced people and unbalanced spirits in need of healing. This ultimately results in power struggles for control, separation, division, competition and eventually war with other people and groups judged as a threat to their power and control. It can even lead to possessions by the unbalanced and unhealed spirits.

How does the leader of the group or those within it recognize the presence of imbalance or spirits in need of healing if they themselves are unbalanced and unhealed? They can't. They don't have the reference points. **Unconditional love without judgment, with the main focus on healing imbalances, will draw balanced people, teachers, healers and the Highest Consciousness and Energy.** This is the path, and the leaders must open the door by healing themselves.

How do you measure the spirituality and intent of a group and its leaders? You know what love is. You know what joy is. You also know what empowers you, lifts you and heals you. You know when your divine right to free will and self-determination is being honored and when you are free to fulfill your own unique purpose. These are tools for discernment in any relationship. You also know what fear, intimidation, judgment, dependencies, separation, competition and self-aggrandizement are, as well as the power struggles for control. It's quite simple: Trust your feelings, and do not allow them to be invalidated.

In conclusion, learn to balance your energies, heal your inner child, focus on love and joy, and forgive your parents if they did not give you a healthy self image. Find the ideal within self and become a sacred man or woman. You will draw to you someone of like mind and begin the journey into a sacred relationship.

Create a sacred relationship with the rest of Humanity and Nature. Honor the Universal Principles, and in doing so you will have a sacred relationship with GOD, for GOD is Humanity and Nature. Treat your mate as a unique and exquisite expression of GOD.

You have to keep loving, no matter how much it hurts, for only by loving all the way through do you gain freedom.

Isis

Sympathetic Resonance and The Law of Attraction

Understanding sympathetic resonance and the law of attraction will help in depersonalizing and coping with the many changes that will occur during the vibrational lifting. There is also the law of repulsion, which will also be covered.

You are all known throughout the universe by your vibration. Your vibration consists of your attitudes, emotions and beliefs about the world in which you live. This has all been formed through experience, and the attitudes, emotions and beliefs gained from these experiences cover many lives, many planes and many dimensions. They are held within what is known as your auric field.

All thought has a vibration. Unconditional love, joy and peace are thoughts of the highest vibration. Fear, anger, jealousy, etc., are thoughts of the lowest vibration. There have been many wounds, traumas, and wrong conclusions from past experiences, which have allowed many lower vibrational attitudes and emotions to be held within one's fields, mixed in with the higher vibrational attitudes and emotions, the truth of one's being. The combination or mixture of the lower vibrational with the higher vibrational attitudes and emotions together establishes one's vibration.

Those who have healed and released the past and choose to express lovingly, joyously and harmoniously are very high vibrational beings. On the contrary, those who choose to express fear, anger and disharmony are very low vibrational beings. There are a lot of in-between and occasional expressions from the highest to the lowest in everyone, yet the majority of the time one usually chooses to express predominantly from the same vibration or level of consciousness.

Sympathetic attraction is when people resonate at the same vibration and are attracted to each other. They will feel an attraction to each other because they are in vibrational sympathy. They are often divine mirrors for each other, reflecting everything they love and hate about themselves. People seldom own the reflection, and so they blame the other; yet if you were attracted to each other and came together through sympathetic resonance, you both share the same attitudes and emotions to one degree or another. **The law of attraction states that we magnetize people and events into our daily lives according to our consciousness.** This is also done according to our vibration. *There is another law known as the law of repulsion, which states that we will repel those who are of a dissimilar or unlike attraction.*

So what does this all have to do with the vibrational lifting? **You are all being vibrationally lifted. Some are moving much faster than others. People will come and go in your lives because you are no longer in sympathetic resonance.**

In some cases, the law of repulsion will make it hard or even impossible to be around some friends, family members and lovers. There will be some friends who will continue in your lives, and your new vibration will also attract other new friends. The friends that are true friends will always be there. They may not understand some of what you are going through, but they will continue to be your friends.

Your biological family will remain, yet family will have a whole new meaning. Your definition of family will continue to expand, taking in new members in a spiritual family. Even the word "home" will take on a new meaning. **Eventually all Humanity will be your family, and beyond that the universal family comes into play, which may include friends on other planes and dimensions as well.** Your home, which was limited to a piece of land with a house on it, extends its boundaries, and Earth becomes your home. You will also eventually go beyond Earth, and the whole universe will become your home. This all comes with an expansion in consciousness and a vibrational lifting.

Those of a higher vibration will seek out others of like mind. They will seek out high vibrational places where the psychic turbulence and lower vibrational attitudes and emotions of social consciousness do not intrude upon their own consciousness. Most of these places are in nature or in sanctuaries that have established the Higher Consciousness and Energy necessary to allow them to expand in consciousness and feel the higher vibrations of pure, unconditional love, joy, peace and freedom. There will be those who come to these places to remember, to recharge and rejuvenate their souls, and take it back to the cities.

There will also be those for whom, though they may enter the cities from time to time in service or for their material needs, the cities will not be their homes. They will choose to remain away from the cities, no matter what the cost, for their priorities and values are different. They know that consciousness is the one eternal gift valued beyond any Earthly treasures. They will gather together. Living a loving, joyous, peaceful life in freedom in a location that is supportive to an expanded consciousness is their first priority. These people are of a very high vibration. They are lovers of life; they will be the mystics, the visionaries, and will have the contacts of which many dream.

It is said that **many are chosen, yet few choose.** These are the ones that did choose; thus they will be rewarded by the very Source itself, along with those in service to the Source. They will be lifted and healed, and heavens shall open for these courageous, steadfast souls. They will become the hands and feet of GOD.

Addicted to Chaos

We have spoken of those going in one direction; now let us discuss those going in another direction.

There are many people who are addicted to chaos, confusion and drama, and some even need multiple dramas all going on at once. They do not have the reference points to live a loving, joyous, peaceful, cooperative existence, and when one is offered to them, they will do everything possible to sabotage it. Why? Because what they have grown accustomed to and feel secure with is the chaos, the confusion and the drama. They will enter one relationship after another with the same reoccurring theme. It is a compulsive behavior pattern. If there is not enough chaos, confusion and drama, they will create it.

What they are experiencing may have no basis in reality, yet they will hold on to their illusion and defend it to the death if necessary. If the ones they have chosen do not wish to participate in the drama, those addicted to chaos will often leave to find someone who will. They will also take with them all of their fears, insecurities and compulsive behavior patterns.

To be in a very loving, supportive, cooperative relationship is often very boring and sometimes very scary to those addicted to chaos. It is like living in a foreign land, the unknown, because they have no reference points. It is completely alien to the life they have grown accustomed to, even though their lives may have been filled with one tragedy after another.

Peace is also very threatening. There is a saying, "Still waters run deep." When one quiets the mind and settles down, his or her spirit has a chance to come forward. It is the true nature of Humanity to be loving and to be at peace.

As spirit begins to rise from the depths of your being, it pushes to the surface those patterns and issues that have been buried, ignored, denied and left unresolved. Those addicted to chaos will have difficulty meditating or being still, because having to reflect upon their past is scary business.

It is unnatural to war, struggle for power, compete, or bring harm to anyone in any way. This includes participating in all the chaos, confusion and dramas, which are not loving and do not bring you joy and peace. It goes against your soul's true purpose and the God self.

Settling down and quieting the mind also threatens the alter ego, because it will have to look at the reoccurring patterns. It will have to own up to the self-created realities and also may have to give up some of its control to spirit. That in itself is also very scary. Again it is the unknown.

Realigning and surrendering to the spirit within is no longer an option upon this plane. It is imperative to align with the Higher Consciousness and Energy and make conscious contact with your own inner guidance and your own inner healer. There are radical changes coming in the land, as well as in consciousness. Those who are addicted to chaos, confusion and the dramas, traumatic

> *Realigning and surrendering to the spirit within is no longer an option upon this plane.*

as they may be, will have their addictions fulfilled a thousand-fold. It will all be amplified, accelerated and the dramas will become very, very dramatic until they have had enough. If they want to continue upon this plane, their only option left is to own their creations, surrender to the God within them and pray that they heal gracefully.

Realigning with and surrendering to the God self, making a commitment to love and peace, will create miracles. Choosing a healing process that works for you will give you the opportunity to heal on your terms in a safe and controlled environment. These are the only options that are now available.

Choosing the option to remain in denial and continue in the chaos, confusion and dramas, which do not correspond with love and peace, will result in very serious consequences. Even death is an option; those who choose that option will continue in their learning and healing process on another plane, another dimension, another school, somewhere else in the universe.

Being a blessing to life and being a channel for love and joy are also options. It is highly recommended that you exercise these two options. You are loved either way unconditionally, yet you will reap what you sow. The choice is up to you.

Facing the Beast

Contrary to popular belief, enlightenment is not comfortable. It is like a birth with many pains, the ultimate of which is the birth of enlightenment itself. Part of this pain is facing your beast.

The beast is like a giant dragon with many heads. It also has a lot of little creations of its own that you will have to conquer before you encounter the beast. It is portrayed in many mythological stories. The hero has to go through many trials and tribulations and slay a few beasts before he can reap the bounty, enter or inherit the kingdom, and claim his reward. The reward usually consists of a beautiful maiden, a treasure or some spiritual, highly prized object that will grant him some form of power.

The adventure of enlightenment is very similar. You choose a path, slay your beast, reunite with your masculine or feminine principle, access a higher power, along with a few tools and techniques, and inherit the kingdom.

You each have a beast that you must face. It is your main unresolved issue that you have chosen to conquer this life. It can often be reduced to one or two words which are the core issue. It could be the beast of betrayal, the beast of unworthiness, the beast of jealousy, the beast of lack, the beast victims call upon themselves, or a whole host of false beliefs and wrong conclusions from past experiences.

Some incarnate to face more than one beast, or combinations, which would be the beast with many heads. Nonetheless, each has his own beast or beasts, and they all must be faced and conquered before moving on into the Christ Consciousness.

Each one of these beasts is based upon fear and unworthiness. These two base issues have created many experiences throughout your eternal sojourns and must be healed. The wisdom must be gained from these experiences in order for it to settle in the soul. If not, the beast only grows larger, returning again and again until the final confrontation.

So how do you slay your beast? You must take full responsibility for your beast. It is your creation. Not taking responsibility, blaming others and denying the existence of your beast only empowers it.

You magnetize people and events into your life according to your consciousness. If you claim to be a victim, your beast will victimize you again and again. If you blame others and project your beast upon them, your beast will still be out there, out of your control, waiting to come through another. **There is only one way out, and that is in. Go within.**

The beast was never outside of you; that was only its projection. It is like fighting a projected image or a hologram. You will never win, and your efforts will be in vain until you take out the projector.

There is a great light within coming through you. That great light begins as the perfect incarnation. If allowed to flow through you unobstructed, it would create a loving, joyous, abundant life, in a whole and healthy body, on a whole and healthy planet. The light must pass through every level of consciousness. You have many subtle bodies endowed with memory, including past life, as well as the mental and emotional bodies, before reaching the physical.

Your physical body is merely coagulated thought, or the hard copy of your attitudes, emotions and beliefs in the world in which you live. You are all creating your bodies and the physical world in which you live, individually and collectively. Now, because I said collectively, this will open the door for many to avoid responsibility and to blame all those other forgotten Gods out there for screwing up their world. Again, YOU magnetize people and events into your lives according to YOUR consciousness. The beast without is the beast within—a projection.

Now here is a little secret known by every Christed Master that walked this plane. We talked about the great light within pressing to manifest. Inherent within that great light is the perfect incarnation. These blocks and patterns, or the little beasties, along with the major beast, exist as thought. It is an energy composed of thought, and it is not physical. Are you getting my drift? If it is not physical, it can be dissolved and healed in consciousness. Your next question is, "How?"

Within each and every one of you is a grand eraser known as the God self. It does not possess an ego to judge right or wrong. It sits patiently like a gentle giant, waiting your command. Its favorite words are, "'AS YOU WISH."

You can command this gentle giant to dissolve your beast, along with all the little beasties. It only needs one thing, and that is to be initiated by you. It does not trespass. It allows you to create all the beasts you want, dissolve all the beasts you want, and loves you unconditionally throughout your entire dramas.

There is another little secret the Masters knew: There is only one mind. They could not only slay their own beasts but the beasts of others by evoking the grand eraser within others. The Masters realized it was a lot of work when others did not take responsibility for evoking their own God selves, for they continued creating beast after beast. They also realized there was an immutable law that honors the divine right to free will and self-determination.

The greatest relief in this knowledge is that the Earth is an action/reaction world known as the plane of demonstration where consciousness creates reality. The action/reaction principle ensures that the lessons will come, with or without the Masters. The beasts will all come home to their creators, and when their creators have had enough pain and suffering, they will eventually have to take responsibility, surrender to their own God selves, and end miscreation.

The Masters are bringing a great light and consciousness to this plane, and it will create a quickening. The beasts will be coming forward and coming home to their creators.

You are entering the days of accountability, responsibility and an end to miscreation. The Beast will have its day;

many shall fall at the hands of their own beast, yet its days are numbered.

There are those in the seen and unseen who will help you face and conquer your beast. Remember, it is by your will, your choice, whether or not you conquer your beast or your beast conquers you. Although you are eternal and time is always optional, the Earth will soon no longer provide that option. It will be a home for the awakened Gods, and the forgotten Gods will continue in another time, another place, another plane. That is how it is now seen.

Between Two Worlds

There is a feeling, or let us say an attitude, that is surfacing throughout the collective consciousness of Humanity. It is a place of understanding where individuals are no longer satisfied with the world in which they live. They know there is something more. They do not know what that something is, yet they cannot continue in their present way of life. It may be their job, their relationship or the society in which they live.

It is a voice, a feeling or a yearning for something else, something grander. There is a deep longing for a truly loving, supportive, cooperative relationship—a love and fellowship that has all of the feelings of young lovers, yet it extends far beyond one's mate, taking in all Humanity and all life. The voice and feeling is getting louder and stronger. It continues to nag and tug at their insides until they can no longer ignore or deny it. It is a grand mirror, showing them what is possible and what does not measure up. The more it is suppressed or resisted, the stronger it becomes. The voice and feeling is your own God self telling you it's time for a change.

It's time to get with the program—you know: the awakening and healing of Humanity and the Earth. That little mission you agreed to before beginning your Earth sojourn. The one you forgot along the way to being a success and making your mark or name in society.

People in all walks of life are awakening. They are leaving unfulfilling jobs and relationships, throwing their positions and social status to the wind, regaining their integrity and making major changes in their lives. They are blowing the minds of their friends and families, shifting gears and starting over in a whole new direction in a divinely inspired march onward into forever.

They have watched the very life force of others fade away. They have seen people spend their entire lives with backs bent and noses to the grindstone. They have watched others, while prostituting themselves and their integrity, climb the ladder of success at the expense of Humanity and Nature, trying to buy happiness. They watch their freedom and the freedom of others diminish as they assimilate more and more into the system.

They have seen through the facades, the empty castles void of love, and decided it was time to leave. Their very souls are screaming at them, saying it's not worth it. There is a better life, a better way of living, a simpler way. They can no longer endure the stress, the chaos, the confusion and the overall lack of love, joy, integrity and fulfillment in their lives.

They want out, and they are getting out, one way or another. Those who choose to leave in the transition called death, when asked if they would do anything different, all agree: "I would have spent more quality time with the people I loved, done more things that bring me joy, and would not have taken life so seriously." If you were to say to them, "Time is money," they would say to you, **"There is no amount of money worth quality time doing something you enjoy with someone you love."**

Many of these people who are between two worlds do not know or understand the new world that is coming, yet they know they can no longer live in the old world. They also feel within themselves that the old world's days are numbered, and a collapse of the old world as they know it is just around the corner. This feeling is surfacing everywhere.

The old world is coming to a close. The Higher Consciousness and Energy will see to its demise, yet it will also usher in the new world. It will be a world of peace and brotherhood; a world where love, unity, cooperation and clean technology will be in order. Love will be the manifesting force behind all creation. It will be a world where GOD, Humanity and Nature find a harmonious balance, a new world that no man can stop, because it is coming from within the hearts and minds of all Humanity.

This shift in consciousness will come at different times to different people. Individuals each have their own divine clock. There are those who are heavily engrossed in the old world, with a strong vested interest, who are very attached to its continuation. There are those who are sitting on the fence, waiting for a little shove in the right direction, a sign, and there are those who

> *Individuals each have their own divine clock.*

have always been different. They have never really completely assimilated into the status quo, and all of their lives they never really felt comfortable or in alignment with society. They are the first to experience the new world, and many are already in it.

This group has strong links with other planes, dimensions and civilizations, which do not experience time as we know it. They are often referred to as Star People, which is an accurate appraisal of the situation. Within their souls they are more from the stars than of Earth, and that memory is coming forward.

They will often have trouble telling you what time it is, what day it is, or remembering events in a chronological order. Something that happened the other day to them may have been three years ago, because they often measure time by the emotions attached to the event. To them it felt like it happened the other day.

It is as if the past, the present and the future are all together. To them, existing in linear time is quite a challenge. You might say they are in this world but not of it. They have trouble comprehending the attitudes, emotions and actions of some people, because to behave in such a manner is beyond them. These ones are very aware that consciousness creates reality, of the action/reaction principle, and treat others and life in all its forms with love and respect. It is inherent within them. It is very hard for them to find reasons for behavior that is not in the highest and best good for all concerned. They are the peacemakers. During the quickening, they will be the first to experience the time distortions.

There have been other civilizations on Earth that went through the same time shift, which are existing right alongside of those within this time flow. The entire Earth is moving into a new time, and linear time will become distorted.

Spirit is not subject to linear time. Your own spirit can go backward or forward in time, and as you become more united with spirit, you will not be as limited. The physical body will also follow suit, becoming more etheric, or what is termed more of an energy body. When this occurs, the rules will change concerning time, distance and space. That is why so many are spacing out, having time distortions and finding it hard to function within the limitations of society. They are expanding, becoming more unlimited, remembering a past not restricted to linear time, and are entering the New Age, much to the chagrin of their peers. They are the pioneers who are courageous enough to usher in a new consciousness, a new time and a new world.

In Greater Hands

There comes a time in your evolution when you realize there is much more to you than your present identity.

Many of you are born into families and feel different from them all throughout your lives. Others awaken later in life and also find themselves very different from the rest of their family. There are those who feel alienated from society in general and cannot comprehend nor desire becoming part of the herd of social consciousness. There are those who have a very hard time fitting in, are very misunderstood and find their present environment very lacking in love, compassion and understanding, and remember another way, another time when things were different.

Deep within their souls, there is a longing to return to that other time or place. They remember a time or place where they were greatly loved and appreciated, and lived in a society that shared in a brother/sisterhood that was far beyond their present relationships. They remember a father or mother who loved them unconditionally, accepted them for who they were, and approved of them as they were. They knew they could always count on their love and understanding. They remember the feeling of being loved, accepted and befriended by others in a way far beyond anything in their present reality. They may remember a time of abundance when life was easier, a time when the struggles for power and greed did not exist. Deep within their hearts, they long to return to those times.

These longings and feelings come for many reasons. There are those who have experienced these feelings in past lives. It is all recorded in their souls as emotions.

There are those who have lived on other planes, dimensions and universes. Some have lived in very spiritually, artistically and technologically advanced civilizations. *There are some who have family in the stars and in the heavens that love them far beyond anything they have ever experienced on Earth.* There are those who remember that love to one degree or another and are very saddened when they measure that love with the love they receive on Earth. They find their parents, lovers, friends and family to fall very short of the feelings they once knew.

Many find the way most of Humanity interacts with each other and their environment unbearable. Some of the attitudes, emotions and actions of some people on Earth are not even within their reality. Many of them feel very alienated, and for good reason. Maybe within their soul they are more alien to the Earth than others. Maybe they came from a distant star or galaxy where life was different.

Maybe they came from a more advanced civilization, and the memory lies deep within them. It could even be possible that they came to Earth to bring that greater awareness to help in service to Humanity and the Earth. They bring an expression of a greater love, another way to interact with Humanity and the Earth.

Maybe we should listen to them rather than shove them into the same little boxes and patterns which have neither served us, Humanity or Nature in the past. Rather than diminish their love and joy and limit their gifts, why not accept them for who they are and what they have to offer?

Why not accept yourself for who you truly are and what you have to offer? Why not come out of the closet, despite the whole of the world? Go beyond the need for acceptance and approval, and own your Divinity! Let the love, joy, wisdom and gifts come forward. Call forth the memories and live them.

There is not one soul who has not experienced a greater love, joy, wisdom and a life of limitless possibilities, because that is the origin of every soul. It's time to unlock those memories, embrace and live them.

Forgive all those journeys into limitation and all those who did not measure up. Forgive your father, your mother, your sister, your brother, friends and lovers who cannot remember. They did the best they could with what they could remember.

Embrace a greater love. There is a whole universe waiting to embrace you, as well as lovers, friends, family, mothers and fathers from the past who loved you greatly and still do. There are always greater hands waiting to embrace you, some of whom have watched over you for eons.

Purpose and Destiny

Each and every one of you has chosen to incarnate during these exciting times. You each have a unique purpose and have chosen to have experiences to help you evolve and heal many of the wrong conclusions from past experiences. You often choose to work with loved ones, as well as those who wronged you and those you wronged in the past.

Past life karma is in the past. The law of forgiveness and grace can heal those unresolved issues in a moment and bring you into the current now. Once you have cleaned up the past, you can move on to a bigger agenda.

There is a master teacher and healer within all of you. It is unique, and has different talents and abilities. It has a purpose, and that purpose is to aid in the awakening and healing process. Until one aligns with this master teacher and healer, there will always be sadness, loneliness and unfulfillment. Despite all the facades and the outer appearances, inside you will be unhappy.

It is only through aligning with one's own God self, committing to and acting upon the pulses which inspire, lift and empower the individual, that one truly finds happiness. There is also a security and bliss that comes with the package. It is not an outer security, nor a happiness based upon the touchstones. It is an internal and eternal security and bliss. Those who have found this sleep very well at night, because they know that their attitudes, emotions and actions of the day were in alignment with their soul's purpose and the God within them. Their lives are directed towards the highest and best good of Humanity and the Earth; therefore they are at peace with themselves.

An individual's purpose and destiny is often in conflict with the world in which he or she lives. The world is constantly changing, and much of it is living in the past. There are systems, codes and doctrines. There are scientific dogmas, religious dogmas and outdated laws and regulations,

---

most of which are obsolete. *It is often one's purpose to usher in a new way of thinking and behaving or entirely different goals and directions in these arenas.* You can find your comfort zone and flow with the status quo, but in doing so you will be cut off from the Higher Consciousness and Energies. The Higher Consciousness and Energies are necessary to heal the sadness, the loneliness, the lack of fulfillment and the very body itself. In other words, by not aligning with the Higher Consciousness and Energies, you will eventually die a sad, lonely, unfulfilled death.

Did you know that death is the failure to live? Did you know that love and joy is the life force? It is what sustains and holds you together. Did you know that the lack of love, joy and fulfillment in your life is the reason you die?

Have you heard of the walking dead? It is called social consciousness. It is those who are not manifesting their own destiny, those who are reacting to the demands of the world in which they live. It is those whose identities and self-esteem are dependent upon outer appearances and the acceptance and approval of their friends, families and lovers. It is those who move with the opinion of the herd, and those who have forgotten individual freedom. They are very insecure, very dependent, and they are tapped into a consciousness filled with fear, unworthiness, doubt, anger and violence and riddled with the attitudes and emotions that create the diseases that are becoming plagues upon the land. That is why these individuals are going to die.

Did you know that within you lies the ability to heal in a moment? Your body also has the ability to live forever. Your scientists are on to this. They have taken the cells within the body and put them in a stress-free environment, and when given proper nourishment, they live forever.

Consciousness creates reality, and aligning with the Higher Consciousness and Energy creates a greater reality. The pure, unconditional love, joy, power and wisdom that come with this Higher Consciousness and Energy will heal the body and bring to you a more loving, joyous, prosperous life. Security and bliss are also part of the package. You must, however, let go of the old consciousness and conquer your fears of change and the unknown.

It is also wise to simplify. **Prosperity and peace of mind often come through simplicity.** Take a few moments each morning or evening and call forward your own God self. Ask that your true soul's purpose be revealed to you. Ask that the doors open and that you be shown the way. When the knowledge comes, have the faith and the courage to walk through the doors.

Prosperity and peace of mind often come through simplicity.

It is an onward journey, sometimes filled with trials and tribulations, that eventually ends in security and bliss—a security and bliss that is eternal, for it is within. Friends and lovers will come and go, things will rot and rust, but your security and bliss will be forever.

Find yourself, your purpose; own and act upon it despite the whole of the world. Live for your feelings. Use your heart, not your head. Let love be your guide, not fear. Only then will you find true security and happiness. If you settle for a comfort zone, you will die, and your consciousness at death determines where you go in your next understanding.

The facades are all coming down. The misalignments and relationships which are based upon a false love or on insecurity will come to an end. Unfulfilling jobs and positions that are out of alignment with your true purpose will also come to a close. There is true love, true security, true purpose, true bliss. It is by your choice, your will, whether you align with it.

We would highly recommend each and every one of you to take stock of your lives. Look at your present predicament, your past, and your present state of consciousness, which determines your future. There is a great, courageous, wise and noble captain in each of you, and it would behoove you to ask just who is steering your ship.

Responding to the Call

There is a forward march currently underway. **People everywhere are responding to a call, a deep feeling to move forward. It is a feeling that they are here for a grander purpose.**

They are often held back by duty, responsibility or fears and insecurities. Little by little the fears and insecurities are falling away. **They are realizing the true definition of responsibility, which is to respond to their soul's purpose despite the whole of the world.** They are finding the courage, self-authority and self-discipline within themselves necessary to complete their unique purpose. A greater awareness of that purpose is also coming forward along with a healthy self-esteem. A strong connection with their own inner guidance, so as not to be swayed by the desires and opinions of others, is also emerging. They are realizing that everyone is his or her own soul. They are owned by GOD and themselves. They are responsible for themselves and accountable to themselves.

Along this forward march there will be many who will try to drag others into their dramas. They will try to make others responsible for their self-created realities. They will use blame, guilt and sympathy, and tell others it is their duty and responsibility to save or care for them. They do not own their self-created realities and do not gain the wisdom from the experience and evolve. Those who ignore the call choose devolution, or to be stuck in reoccurring patterns and playing victim roles, dragging saviors and persecutors into their triangle in endless dramas.

The saviors are also responding to the call. They have had enough of being victimized by the very ones they set out to save, or having the role of persecutor projected upon them. They are realizing when help is truly help, and not perpetuating the role of victim. They are holding the victims accountable and responsible for their self-created realities, putting an end to their part of the drama.

Even the persecutors are running out of victims, turning inward upon their own wounds and traumas that they are vicariously working out through the victims. **The ones making the most progress on this forward march are the ones who are learning to allow.** They are focused upon their own awakening and healing process. On this forward march you will have to release many within your family, your friends and lovers who do not wish to take the journey. They will become a drain of energy, and try to drag you back into a comfort zone that is familiar to them. In some cases, they will war upon your own evolution, casting doubt or fear upon your forward march into enlightenment.

Those who tarry and choose fear and doubt or continue in the wars, dramas and dilemmas of social consciousness will be left to themselves and their self-created realities. Their fears, insecurities, judgments, condemnations and all separative lower vibrational attitudes and emotions will manifest.

Eventually, when they have had enough, they will remember a friend, the one who taught by example. They will remember the one who allowed them their path, yet remained steadfast on his or hers. They will pack their bags and answer their own call. You will have shown them the strength and courage necessary to begin their forward march into forever.

Critical Mass

There is a well-known story concerning the hundredth monkey, which demonstrates group mind, or the collective consciousness of a species, and how all those within a species are connected, regardless of geographical location.

The story, in short, begins with a monkey that decides to start washing its sweet potatoes. Another monkey observes the act and begins to wash its sweet potatoes, then another and another begins, until the hundredth monkey

---

decides to wash its sweet potatoes. After the hundredth monkey, all the other monkeys which were separated on other islands washed their sweet potatoes. Critical mass was reached when that hundredth monkey decided to wash his or her potatoes, which made it customary within the group mind or collective consciousness of the monkeys to wash their potatoes.

Each species has a group mind or collective consciousness, including Humanity. What is done by the one affects the many, and if enough follow suit, eventually critical mass will be reached, and it will be customary to behave accordingly.

By now we hope this understanding has inspired a light within your own consciousness. A question you might ask is, "What would happen if I lived a path of honesty and integrity, and governed my life according to universal principles and understandings?" What if I started loving unconditionally, and began allowing and honoring the sacred circle of life? What if another was to observe me, and another and another, and they too chose the same path? What if enough were to choose the same path?

The most powerful consciousness in the universe is love and joy; what if enough of us aligned ourselves with this energy? What would it do to the group mind or collective consciousness of Humanity?

What if I connected with other planes and dimensions where they have chosen as a collective to align themselves with this same consciousness and energy? What if I become a vibrational bridge or channel for their consciousness and energy upon this plane? What if another observed me, and they learned to also be a channel for this same consciousness and energy, and another and another, and we all held steadfast in our new understanding? What effect would that have on the collective consciousness?

A profound effect happens, one that some day will reach critical mass and eventually become a way of life. A path of honesty, integrity and noble virtue is very fashionable.

Unconditional love, joy and service to Humanity and the Earth are also very contagious attributes. This is happening on a grand scale, individually and collectively.

There are groups and whole communities which have chosen this path around the world, inspired by the heavenly hosts. Critical mass is not far away. The base resonant frequency of Earth has risen from 7 megahertz to over 8, and is rapidly moving to 12.

The Earth and those who reside upon her are moving into a new time, a higher frequency which resonates with a Higher Consciousness and Energy. We are on our way home. It is the Golden Age of GOD, in thanks and deepest gratitude to the meek. They are in alignment, and they are the examples, the potato washers that started a trend which launched Humanity into a new age. They will be known by name in the book of life, in the greatest of halls, by the grandest of masters, as the bravest of Angels who endured.

GOD Is a Feeling

GOD is a feeling, a deep, profound feeling. GOD is not found in sacred books, yet books can trigger the feelings. GOD is not found in churches, yet churches can inspire the feelings. GOD is not in the prayer or the meditation, yet both can help you feel the presence of GOD.

All the intellectual rhetoric, the doctrines, the rituals, the "isms," etc., without deep, profound feelings are distractions. All the philosophies, the phrases, the repeating of scriptures, quotes, new age lingo, old age lingo, etc., without feelings are dead. Many who take the path of the intellect without feelings become the walking dead. Even their God is dead, unfeeling and somewhere in the past.

There are heart people and head people. Heart people live by their feelings. They can access the nature of a person in a moment. Those who can feel profoundly can walk by a person and know all there is to know about that person, in a moment! They can feel a person's present mental state, know their intentions, and know their tomorrow, because their tomorrow is created by their present mental state.

Some heart people can feel what is happening with friends, lovers and family, wherever they reside. Those with deep, profound feelings can feel what is happening everywhere upon the planet. They can feel other planes and dimensions; some are sensitive to the entire universe. There could be a natural disaster on the planet or a war in another galaxy, and it would be felt. That is how far-reaching feelings can be. GOD is omnipresent, omniscient feelings.

Those who are one with GOD are deep feeling entities. They can attune and feel anything, anywhere in the universe. Their feelings will tell them all they need to know. That is the nature of those who align themselves with the one consciousness that encompasses all consciousness.

The most powerful and far-reaching feelings are love and compassion. Joy and peace are also feelings that reach out into forever. These feelings are of the highest vibration. There are other lower vibrational feelings that cause individuals to close down, contract and become inaccessible to God and the very life force necessary to maintain their physical well-being.

Let us talk about those who cannot feel. There are many who are bottled up in their emotions. They have either been very wounded in the past or have gotten into a mundane rut, a relationship or a job that is very lacking in love, joy and fulfillment. There is a grayness to them, and they are often stuck in routines that are very unstimulating. Many of their lives consist of going to work, coming home and plopping down in front of the TV, grabbing a beer, washing the car and mowing the lawn on Sunday, followed by another beer and a football game. They depend upon the newspaper, the TV and the local gossip for all of their information. They have the house, the family, the new car and all that it takes to measure up to the standards set by society to be successful. They are attuned to and reacting to social consciousness, a consciousness with very little joy, inspiration and love, that is not very expanded. They have become numb to deep, profound feelings and are very unemotional. The passion is gone from their lives, and these are the ones we refer to as the walking dead.

Did you ever wonder why teenagers rebel so animatedly? They are alive and free, and do not want to end up trapped in the same cage as their parents. They can see the absence of love, joy, passion and freedom. It is what every new generation rebels against. There are other reasons concerning establishing their own identity; yet if they were truly satisfied with the lives and identity of their parents, there wouldn't be so much rebellion.

Let us now talk about emotions. **It is through powerful emotions that everything came into being. It is why you are here on the Earth: to master powerful emotions.** The power to manifest comes from embracing something passionately with powerful emotions.

> *You are here on the Earth to master powerful emotions.*

The Christ Consciousness is where GOD knows self to be man/woman, and man/woman knows self to be GOD. Before the union can occur, all of the blocks, patterns and wrong conclusions that block deep, profound feelings and powerful emotions must be healed and released.

Jesus represented this when he tore up the marketplace and drove out the money changers. It was a process. It was his deep, profound love, admiration and respect for GOD, embraced with powerful emotions, that drove him to do what he did. He did not care what people would think. He didn't ask the permission of the priests. He responded to the feelings and powerful emotions within him.

Some may say it was an irresponsible act, yet **responsibility means responding to the feelings and powerful emotions within.** He also did it fearlessly. It was quite a sight to see. He did not feel guilty after doing it, either. It was a great release, and they laughed about it later. Later he grew to love even the money changers and those who profit using the favor of GOD to sell their wares. The wares will sell of their own merit if they are worth anything.

Becoming a pure channel for deep, profound feelings and emotions is being a channel for GOD. Embrace your desires passionately and emotionally, allowing GOD to manifest through you.

Aligning with your soul's purpose and destiny, embracing it passionately, fearlessly, with powerful emotions, is a powerful and exhilarating experience. Having the love, joy, power and wisdom of GOD at your disposal is also a grand experience. Remaining steadfast and committed to that purpose, often against all odds, takes a lot of courage, self-acceptance and self-worth. You have it all within you.

When the deep, profound feelings and the powerful emotions come, do not block them. Do not judge the feelings and emotions as inappropriate and unacceptable, lest you become the walking dead. Do not retreat into an intellectual shell, disregarding them as something unholy. Own them, process, heal and release them. Do not stuff and stifle them. They will only grow stronger and consume you.

There will be a lot of raging in the days to come. Everyone has his or her money changers and marketplaces. Some will rage against their fathers, their mothers, their bosses, their friends, lovers or the system, and all the injustices done to them will surface. They will also project these upon others.

Jesus said when asked if he was the bringer of peace, "Yes, but first I bring a sword." He also said, "I will turn daughters against their mothers, sons against their fathers and men against men." This is a process necessary to heal and release the blocks, patterns, wounds, traumas and wrong conclusions from past experiences.

Some will even rage at GOD. They will say, "How could life be so unfair? Why is GOD doing this to me?"

GOD is allowing you to do as you wish, to yourself, to

others, etc. GOD is only amplifying, quickening, manifesting and magnetizing people and events into your daily lives according to your consciousness. Your attitudes, emotions and beliefs in the world in which you live are your consciousness.

It's being done with a deep, profound, powerful emotion called love. It is a feeling that is coming forward within everyone; a sword before the peace. We can surrender to the sword and heal gracefully, or continue to resist feeling the full impact, the pain and the suffering of self-inflicted wounds, self-created realities. It is as you wish, and you will be greatly loved through all of your manifestations.

Surrender your burdens to love. Allow the profound feelings to come forward. Learn to cry, to weep and to feel the love and joy underneath the sorrow and tears. Expect a miracle.

I only know what I feel, and what I experience, and how that experience feels. When I learn to trust those feelings, I trust GOD, for GOD is a feeling. That is all I know to be a fact.

The Myth of Money

We are going to take you on a mythological journey concerning the origin of money to give you an understanding of where you are economically and how you got there.

A long time ago people traded for goods and labor using precious gems and metals, or barter. Everything was based upon real value, as one's labor was of real value, food and hard goods were of real value, and the precious gems and metals were also of real value.

The precious gems and metals were weighed and appraised by the goldsmiths and those who new the value of gems. They also became the banks, and gave receipts based on the value of what was given to them to hold. Eventually, rather than going to the goldsmith and picking up one's gems and metals to barter or trade, people found it easier to trade the receipts for their gems and metals. Thus the first paper money was created. The goldsmiths, because of their receipts, now became the bankers, and realized that they always had a large surplus of gems and gold because very few people needed all of their gems and gold at once. Rather than carry it around, it was safer for them and their gold for the goldsmiths, which we will refer to as bankers from this point on, to keep it.

Soon the bankers' vaults were overflowing with surplus and the threat of war was escalating with another country. The bankers went to the King and said, "We will loan to you at a slight interest the gems and gold you need to buy the arms necessary to win the war. It will be in the form of a receipt, but you must declare these receipts as legal tender in order for you to acquire what you need to win the war." The King agreed, and now the receipts were legal tender, backed by precious gems and gold.

The King won the war and pillaged the country he conquered of its precious gems and gold, bonded the remaining men into slavery and stole their women. The bankers made a tidy profit, for the King paid them back in precious gems and gold, plus interest. All they had to do was print up some receipts. They did not have to labor, or trade anything of real value, and their time and energy concerning the venture was little or nothing. This went very well for the bankers. The King also expanded his kingdom and made a profit, and the army got a shekel or two and a lot of wine and women from the land they conquered.

Things settled down for a little while, and the bankers, remembering how well it went the last time, decided it was time for another war. They went to another bordering King and told him war was afoot, and they would finance him to buy the arms he needed to win. They even paid bandits to dress up as the opposing side and attack the King's men.

The King was outraged, and agreed to borrow the money to buy the arms needed to conquer his opposition, again in the form of receipts, yet this time the bankers sold him the arms also, at a tidy profit. The new receipts had to be different, because now they were in a different country. The King also needed to buy food and materials in his country as well; therefore a decree was passed making the receipts legal tender.

Again the war was fought and won, and the bankers made an enormous profit using their receipts, which were now accepted currency in two countries. The King paid them back from the spoils of war, again in precious gems and metals. Even though precious gems, metals or anything of value were never given—only receipts—the bankers were always repaid in precious gems and metals. Now their receipts were standard currency in two countries, and they could trade for labor, food, clothing and any other commodities, as well as precious gems and metals, for their receipts. They did not have to labor or toil, nor did they have to trade anything of real value to acquire everything they needed.

Even though they lived a prosperous and abundant life, their unbridled greed and lust for power fueled them to continue. They even created wars within the countries they had profited greatly from in the past. They knew that now they could sell arms to both sides, print more receipts, and eventually get all of the precious gems and gold from one king or the other, depending upon who was victorious. No matter which side won, the bankers always came out ahead.

The kings were always envious of each other's countries, their gold and their women, and the armies were restless and had to be maintained and financed through the spoils of war. War now became a necessity. The bankers played cold-hearted chess with kings and countries, continuing to amass great wealth and power, even at the expense of their own people, for they had no allegiance to anyone. The Gods they worshipped were money and power.

The stakes became higher and higher. The kings had to borrow enormous sums of money to fight the wars, and they could not cover the costs or the interest. The bankers came up with another clever idea, and that was to pass the burden on to the people. After all, it was their country that needed to be protected. They told the King that by taxing the people he could continue to buy arms, support his armies, and even expand his kingdom further, for there were other countries he could conquer that were rich with both human and natural resources.

Taxes were levied to finance the wars, and receipts upon receipts were printed while the bankers, who were now international in their scope, continued to reap the rewards. There were so many receipts out against the goods, labor and precious gems and metals, that the international bankers now owned everything. They loaned out their receipts at high interest and amortized them over years, bonding people into years of indentured service. They controlled the kings and their people through debt, and both lived in fear of having that debt called, even though the debt was invalid, because nothing of value was ever traded from their side.

The kings were coerced into giving up much of their ruling power, their land and the natural resources to pay off the debts. Taxes were also raised continuously, placing heavier burdens upon the people. The natural resources were plundered, and the land was divided and sold, bringing more people under the bankers' control through debt, binding the new land owners into indentured service.

The kings and their people, one by one, fell under the clever spell of the international bankers. They took over kingdoms and their people by creating debt, based upon a receipt that had no real value at all. They did not labor. They didn't even own enough gems or precious metals to back up their receipts. All they did was print the receipts, get people to believe they were of value, pressure the kings to issue a decree establishing the receipts as an accepted exchange for labor, gems, precious metals and other goods, and loan the receipts out at interest, amortizing it over the years. Soon they owned and controlled everything.

The receipts are, in truth, as much now as before, worthless pieces of paper backed by the international bankers. To this day, they continue loaning trillions to governments, passing on the debt, plus interest, to the people. They also regulate taxes to pay off that debt.

In truth, the IRS and the tax collecting agencies in other countries are under their control. The majority of the world is under the spell, governed by nothing more than an idea and a piece of paper. The more a country borrows, the more they own that country, as well as the natural and human resources in that country.

Their unbridled greed and lust for power at the expense of Humanity and Nature demands that you keep your backs bent and your noses to the grindstone. They have manufactured lack as a way of control, and will maintain their positions at any cost. Humanity as a collective is like a frog in the pot. If you turn up the heat a little at a time, the frog never realizes he is having the life boiled out of him until it is too late.

There are three things the tyrants fear. The first is SOVEREIGNTY. If you become sovereign, and not dependent on them for your food, transportation, shelter, utilities and job security, they have no control over you, and you are a threat.

The second is EDUCATION. They are not threatened by the standard curriculum and the recycled ignorance taught in most schools and colleges, especially those designed to maintain the status quo. **They are threatened by the Higher Consciousness, where nothing is hidden, and by those who engage the Higher Consciousness and pass it on.** They can't have their spell broken, and those who rise above social consciousness into the Christ Consciousness are the greatest threat of all. Why? Because an awakened God is very hard to handle. They can't be deceived. They have telepathic abilities and the ability of direct knowing. They know what is in the highest and best good of Humanity and the Earth and the Universal Principles. They know the true goals and intentions of the tyrants; thus they become an immense thorn in their side. They also know Humanity's divine heritage and the light that lighteth every man/woman, which is the light of GOD. Knowledge of the loving, joyous, wise and powerful manifesting God within is the greatest threat of all.

The last threat is ABUNDANCE. They know that money is power. It truly has no power of its own other than what you give it, yet Humanity as a collective has associated money with power. Some abundance is allowed; yet if you become too abundant, you have, in their eyes, too much power. They are sitting upon trillions; therefore a few billionaires and millionaires are not much of a threat, as long as they continue to play their game. **The majority, however, must be kept under their control through manufactured lack and by controlling the lifeline the collective is dependent upon—your food, shelter, transportation, utilities, etc.**

There are other costs governed by them, including taxes, and through these dependencies they reign over Humanity. It's their system. *As long as their receipts, "money," are the controlling factor governing destiny and they control the money, Humanity individually and collectively will stagnate in evolution.*

Reason this: They do not want you to become sovereign, abundant or educated beyond the standard curriculum and recycled ignorance, which maintains the status quo. How can you evolve and reach your greatest potential? What happens to the geniuses? They are locked up, shut up, or end up employed by the government, and all they have to offer is under lock and key, in the interest of national security.

If those within our government consider themselves a separate nation, as well as the special interests that govern them, this I understand. It is not in their highest and best good to give the people free energy, transportation which runs on electricity fueled by perpetual motion magnetic generators, frequency generators and radionic devices that would end disease with the flick of a switch, or abundance; especially if through abundance, people had the free time to think, allowing their own genius to come forward. That is why you evolve very slowly.

You are kept very busy surviving, chasing those little pieces of paper to make ends meet in confusion, and mesmerized by your drugs, alcohol and TV. As long as Humanity remains ignorant and complacent, the international bankers will continue to reign, and evolution will be retarded. It's time to wake up!

What is sad is that now they don't even have to print the money. It's all done electronically, and what you receive from your labor and how much of it you can keep is all done electronically. Your time, energy, indebtedness and destiny are all determined by numbers punched into a keyboard. This includes your transportation and the acquisition of shelter, food and clothing. They give you a debit card linked to a computer, yet few have contemplated just who controls the computer or what happens if your card is invalidated.

Reason this: Of what value is an electronic promise? Who made the promise, and established value to a piece of paper and an electronic digit? Can either stand on their own as something of value? What happens when the spell is broken? What if the power grid fails, which is destiny? Are you just going to stand there dumfounded, card in hand, with no food, water, shelter and power? You will have toilet paper, because you can use those little green pieces of paper.

Those who do not wake up are going to find themselves very dependent, very controlled and in a very precarious position when the spell is broken and the curtain comes down. It is coming down. There are no longer enough human or natural resources to exploit in order to continue business as usual.

This next understanding concerns honesty, integrity and the selling of one's soul for these printed pieces of paper and electronic debit cards. It is said that every man has his price. (This includes women also.) What is sad is that for a large part of Humanity this is true. You sell out your friends, your families, your lovers, your country and your souls, all for a few pieces of paper someone told you was worth something.

The international bankers know this and depend upon it. They know that for a specific amount of money, a title or a position, the majority of you will do their bidding. You will turn upon your own people, destroy your environment, go to war, and sell your bodies for the sense gratification of the wealthy, all for a few pieces of paper with numbers printed on them. It's amazing!

Has anybody ever questioned how unconscious and idiotic that is? If I were to grab a few pieces of paper, write a few numbers on them, and tell you I will trade you them for your car, your house, your land, your labor, your body, would you do it? What if I told you I would give them to you if you will turn on your neighbor, enslave them through debt, go to war, or destroy your environment? It's an every-day occurrence.

Honesty, integrity and noble virtue have their price, and the international bankers are willing to pay it. Those they can't own they often publicly humiliate, destroying them financially or physically if necessary. Of course, they won't do it themselves. Why should they, when they can get someone else to do it for them? Their resources in these areas are unending. They control governments, politicians, enforcement agencies, collection agencies, including the IRS, and have their own people as well to do their bidding. They even own the Federal Reserve, which is a private corporation which maintains the status quo of manufactured lack.

They know that all they have to do is give you a title, a position with a little power and a paycheck, and you will do just about anything, especially if you depend upon that paycheck for security. The grander the title, the more power that comes with the position and the larger the paycheck, the more you will do their bidding. The more you maintain the status quo, the more you become just like them. There are a lot of little mini-tyrants out there just like them on a smaller scale. "We" is not in their vocabulary, unless it includes those they control and who will do their bidding.

They believe material acquisitions and outer appearances establish character and self-worth. Their self-worth also depends upon how many they govern, and they do not care how many backs they step upon to rise above the masses, who dies or how they impact the environment.

They are seeking love, acceptance and approval, and are trying to establish self-worth through material acquisitions, outer appearances, positions and the overpowering of others. You know: the car, the castle, the clothes, the title and the rest of the props. They are so busy trying to acquire love, respect, acceptance and approval and establish self-worth through material acquisitions and outer appearances that they never take the time to look within themselves. If they loved, respected and approved of themselves, they wouldn't need all the props.

If they valued themselves, they would not need the opinions of others to establish self-worth. The props in most cases are there to make up for what is lacking on the inside. Their entire stock is invested in transitory objects and the opinions of others. When they lose their material acquisitions and outer appearances, self-worth takes a dive. When they lose the approval and acceptance of others, their opinion of self also takes a dive. If their love depends upon the love of another, they again are subject to the ups and downs of the one they love.

If one's identity depends upon outer appearances, material acquisitions or the opinions and love of others, he or she is in for dire straights in the days to come. This includes those who think they can control the destiny of others.

Love always empowers, never overpowers. It serves Humanity and Nature, and is the ultimate power in the universe. It is love that is coming as a great amplifier and accelerator of the action/reaction principle. Those who have not acted in the highest and best good of Humanity and Nature will suffer the reaction at the hands of Humanity and Nature.

There is going to be a lot of transition, a lot of processing and a lot of projection being done, increasing exponentially in the future. Kingdoms will rise and fall, people will come and go, and positions will open and close.

Those who love, accept and approve of themselves, those who simplify and those who are humble enough to listen within and prepare will make it through. They have the honesty, integrity and wisdom to see the ignorance of acting in any way that is harmful to Humanity and the Earth. They will not suffer the reactions fast approaching on the horizon, and their steadfastness will weather any storm. They are the meek, and they are guided. They own eternally what the others are seeking, for it is within them. In that lies their security.

In the days to come, it will be wise to become as sovereign as possible. Educate yourselves, not in the ways of social consciousness and recycled ignorance; go beyond into quantum realities and Higher Consciousness.

The Earth's true history and the origin of man, the way it is taught and understood, bears very little resemblance to the truth. There is more to you and your universe than you will ever experience through standard curricula.

Take time from your labor. Look at the abundance of Nature and the laws of Nature; they are your best teachers. Find yourself a great tree and sit beneath it; a river, a creek or a mountaintop. Go someplace in Nature where you can be alone, away from the psychic turbulence of the city. Get out of social consciousness and contemplate life. Ask yourself why you are not happy. Why do you not feel free? Why don't you know yourself? The answers will come. Ask for clarity.

The Paradox of Power

In the days to come, you are going to see the great paradox unfold. The veils are coming down, and all will be seen as it truly is. **Telepathy and direct knowing will replace relying directly on the five senses.** Everything will be revealed, and nothing will remain hidden. The true goals and intentions, as well as the powers behind the scenes, will be revealed in each individual, each organization and each institution. This includes governments and religious institutions as well.

The facade that is shown to you will in most cases be completely contradictory. Words will not correspond with actions, and **the future is going to get very confusing. The confusion is only the precursor to clarity.** When truth comes forward and that truth is contrary to what we believe, what we were shown or taught, and is contrary to our present reality, there is a struggle. The ego is established, often firmly, and identifies with what is known. When what is known turns out to be false, there is an identity crisis to one degree or another.

There is also the fear of the unknown and of operating outside of the standards of society, which is often met with great resistance. There is also the security of remaining within those standards, because for many their jobs and their very survival depend upon it.

In the days to come, the standards are going to change constantly. People everywhere are going to be put in a position of redefining self and their relationships to others, to their environment and to the very Source itself. You are entering tumultuous times of social, economic and physical Earth changes.

It is a quickening. During this process, tyrants will rise, only to fall. The ministers and their institutions will divide into those who serve GOD and those who serve themselves and their institutions; the selfless and the selfish. Those who continue to extort money in the name of GOD and promote fear, unworthiness, guilt and separation in their lust for power and control will be seen for what they are. Those who stand for peace, unity, love and joy, honor diversity, and love GOD, Humanity and Nature will continue to stand.

The businessmen who exploit both human and natural resources will also be seen for who they are, despite their deceptive ads and campaigns. The politicians who are puppets for special interests will also be revealed. This includes their actions, which bear little or no resemblance to the facade they put forward. The international bankers and their past will be revealed, as well as their plans for the future.

You will see institutions with names and people with titles which sound very noble and forthwith be exposed for actions which are completely contrary to their names, titles and positions. Look at your government. It isn't really your government. It is run by special interests, behind which are the international bankers. Look at the Federal Reserve System. It's not federal; it is a private banking institution which prints money, even though it is strictly forbidden in the Constitution for banks to print money.

How about the Internal Revenue System? It is another private institution governed by the international bankers, which creates and enforces its own laws, again in complete contradiction to the Constitution. They are both private institutions which are unconstitutional and derive their powers from maritime law, not common law.

Look at the FDA. It is run by the major drug companies and those who provide expensive hospital equipment. Is it wise to give them the power to decide the method and cost of a cure? What about the enforcement agencies, which in the interest of national security block or confiscate free energy devices which would end our dependency on foreign oil, not to mention healing devices which would put an end to most diseases?

Look at the welfare system. It creates dependencies, perpetuates the victim role, and promotes division and separation in many cases. It would be better labeled the warfare system, because it is filled with so many people that are working out their own unresolved issues vicariously.

Look at your Forest Service. Wouldn't it be better understood as the Deforest Service? They build the roads and sell the timber, and one only has to look at the massive clearcuts and what is left of our forests to realize a lot more has been taken than has ever been saved. According to their numbers, only 20% of the forest has been cut. They include barren land and mountaintops as forests in their statistics. Fly over them; over 80% has been cut. The greatest service they have rendered is to the major logging operations, at your expense.

How about the crusades, the inquisitions, and the separation, division and religious wars continuing to this day? **More people have died in the name of God than have ever been saved.**

Have you ever heard the words, "We are here to help"? How about, "We are here to protect, provide security and ensure your freedom"? What about, "We care about our environment, and we are here to ensure a better tomorrow"? The latest one is, "We must save them at any expense, especially the children, even if it means killing the lot of them." Who is "we" and who is "them?" What happens when we become them?

Your government, which began as a cute little kitten caged by the Constitution, is now an enormous beast. It's out of its cage, hungry, and cannot be fed enough. You now live in fear of what was created to serve you, and now you are in the cage.

Your forefathers established this country under the Constitution to prevent large oppressive government and over-taxation, and ensure personal and religious freedom, equality and certain unalienable rights to life, liberty and the pursuit of happiness. These rights are endowed by the Creator, and if any government becomes destructive of these ends, it is the right and duty of the people to restructure or abolish that government.

The British have landed! They came in the form of the international bankers, and they didn't even have to fire a shot, other than a few assassinations of those who were on to them. Your forefathers are turning in their graves, because the foundation of your country, and other countries as well, has been invaded and altered to do the bidding of the international bankers.

Many of your forefathers have reincarnated and will

again be a voice for equality, freedom and justice for all. They are going to take on the beast and those who do its bidding. They are a wakeup call that will spread like wildfire in the days to come.

You are going to hear the beast roar. Many will feel its bite and its foul breath. The burden of the beast will be felt by everyone. There shall come a day when the burden and the pain will escalate to the degree necessary for the people to say, "Enough! It is finished."

All will be revealed. As a collective, Humanity will find the courage to make its stand, and the beast will die because no one will fear it or feed its demands. It will be seen for what it is. The few families that control the beast will also be revealed and have to stand before the angry masses. Even their own people will turn upon them.

The Federal Reserve and the Internal Revenue systems will collapse. The national debt which has held Humanity hostage will also be erased. Individual freedom, prosperity and power will return to the people, partially because of the brave souls who took a stand, yet the greatest contribution will be from a grand old lady called Nature.

Also revealed, in the days ahead, will be the complete contradictions in names and actions. What was and is created in name to heal, empower, educate, protect and serve will act in a manner that is contrary in one degree or another to its name. There will be a lot of talk, and very little walk.

Even in the New Thought and metaphysical organizations, there will be power struggles by those who profess unconditional love and to be a channel of the love and life force energies. They are going to have to back up and look at their motives and the driving force behind their actions. Is it love or fear that's driving them? Are they in it for the power and money, or the healing and empowering of all? Are they in fear of losing their following, and does their security depend on the contributions of their following, and on keeping that following under their control? Have they ventured into spiritual ego and self-aggrandizement?

These are questions we must all ask ourselves repeatedly, for the ego is always trying to exalt self above others and seize control. **The paradoxes will come forward and be seen for what they are. People everywhere, individually and collectively, will be known for their true goals and intentions, as well as what is truly in their hearts and minds.** Nothing will be hidden, and no rock will be left unturned.

> *When a person says trust, trust, trust, it's time to count your spoons, spoons, spoons.*
> Confucians

Becoming Gods

2

A Denied Past, Present and Future

Spell of the Enslavers

Have you any idea how much the world in which you live depends upon denial, control and manipulation? If you don't, you are in denial, because it takes an enormous amount of denial, control and manipulation to maintain the world in which you live.

Your jobs, your relationships, your false security; most all depend upon the big three. Your government could not exist without them. Most big businesses could not exist without them. Your very job probably could not exist without them, and most relationships could not stand the scrutiny of brutal honesty. The dependencies in these arenas demand the presence of the big three. **The false security the big three offers is rapidly diminishing, because the big three are in complete conflict with Universal Principles and the Laws of Creation.**

Government and big business are also often in deep conflict with the Universal Principles and Laws of Creation. To simplify the matter, there is one law that supersedes all other laws, and that is the Law of Love.

How many of your laws are in alignment with the Law of Love? How about individual freedom and the divine right to free will and self-determination? How about the action/reaction principle: For every action there is an equal and opposite reaction, and whatever one does to cause pain, suffering or loss to Humanity and Nature, he or she will experience the same in equal measure? How about always acting in the highest and best good for Humanity and the Earth, and forgiveness and compassion? How often do your government, big business and your own personal job stick to these Universal Principles?

What about your relationships? Do you always act in the highest and best good of your mate? Do you act without any expectations or hidden agendas? Be honest now. Are there dependencies, fears, insecurities and other agendas at work? What are your true motives? Can you be brutally honest with yourself?

What are the motives of your governments, your politicians and big business? Are you a part of this game? Are you dependent upon the continuation of this game? Are you, or the business you are in, causing pain, suffering or loss in any way, not acting in the highest and best good of Humanity and the Earth, for the sake of profit and security?

Need a more realistic scenario? What if you are a doctor or a nurse, and a device comes out that will end most disease and make drugs unnecessary? What if the FDA, run by the drug companies, makes it illegal, thus saving your job, which depends upon people being sick? Would you breathe a sigh of relief, and support the government in banning these devices, or use whatever means possible to heal your patients according to your oath?

What if the killer viruses and bacteria ran rampant because of your overtaxed immune systems, and the drugs you now have are rendered useless because of the mutations, which are rendering the viruses and bacteria immune? What if an energy device which can kill any virus or bacteria was put in your hands, as well as the cure for AIDS and cancer? Would you use it? What if it meant you would lose your license, your job, your freedom and maybe your life?

What if the life of your wife, your husband, your children, your mother or father, or your best friend was in your hands? Would you watch them suffer needlessly and die, as those have who suppressed this technology? These devices do exist.

What if you were a psychologist or a psychiatrist, and a person came along schooled in a different way without a prestigious degree? What if they had the ability to intuitively go directly to the source of a person's problem wherever it resided, be it from a past life, birth, childhood or a recent wound, trauma or wrong conclusion from past experience, and heal it there on the spot, without years of therapy? Would you learn from them, putting the well-being of the patient as first priority? Or would you turn them in for practicing without a license, or breathe a sigh of relief when they are shut down by the authorities and ordered to discontinue healing people?

What if you were an orthodox minister, had a large congregation, and the existence of your church depended upon keeping that congregation intact and contributing on a regular basis? Along comes a man or woman who has the ability to heal with a touch, has wisdom far beyond this world, and inspires the people to go beyond the fear, unworthiness and guilt, and become one with the God within them. It is not your temple, but the temple within. What if the religion you belonged to judged, condemned and had this person demonized or put to death? Could you truly continue in good conscience your affiliation with that organization? It has been going on for centuries!

What if you owned a major oil company, provided power to people through gas, oil, coal or electricity, or worked and owned stock in these companies, and along comes a free energy device that will furnish all your energy needs in the home, as well as transportation, for free? Would you help your fellow man become sovereign? Would you again breathe a sigh of relief when your government or big business does away with such a device and the inventor? They have done so in both arenas since the forties.

What if the continuation of Humanity as a species and the very platform for life depend upon these devices coming forward? IT DOES! What if your government has this technology and you came across it, along with a lot of other borrowed technology? Would you have the courage to spill the beans? Many are, and on their death beds those who have been involved in these cover-ups, black operations and projects are having an immense struggle with their own conscience.

As for your relationships, we also have a few questions to ponder in this arena. What if there was very little love, passion and evolution in your relationship, and someone else came along, someone with whom you could experience love, passion and a quantum leap in evolution? What if that someone came along, not for you, but for your mate? Could you be with that someone or love your mate enough to allow him or her to be with that someone? How sovereign are you, and how conditional is your love?

Do you love your mate enough to do what is in the highest and best good for him or her? Can you act for his or her evolution and happiness, even if it means being with another? How much fear, insecurity and dependency is in your relationship? Is it based upon the shoulds and duties of social consciousness?

How about freedom? What about the big three: denial, control and manipulation? How much of them are in your own personal relationship? As you can see, the entire world depends upon the continuation and perpetuation of these very base attitudes and emotions. When you take the big three and add a lot of unbridled greed and lust for power at the expense of Humanity and Nature, what you have is the powers that be which are governing your world. Is it the real world?

When people tell you that you have to be realistic, does that mean you have to live in denial and continue to control and manipulate or be controlled and manipulated? Is that GOD's wish for you? What is real? Is being a decent human being and living a life of honesty, impeccable integrity and service to Humanity and Nature unreal? What about a life without fear, unworthiness, dependency and insecurity? Is a life in alignment with your heart's desires, a life of love, passion and complete freedom, so unreal?

Unfortunately, the world we now live in is "the price is right." Everyone has his or her price, insecurities and attachments which he or she is unwilling to surrender for a greater world. **The greater world is where love and passion can unfold to its greatest heights, individual freedom abounds and the environment thrives.** Unfortunately, there will be a greater price to pay in the long run, because **any world based upon denial, control and manipulation, as well as actions against Humanity and Nature, will not survive.** It has no foundation, and goes against the Universal Principles and the Laws of Creation. History will repeat itself, and **the collapse of your society, your economy and your environment is inevitable without drastic change in all arenas.** Evolution is greatly inhibited upon the Earth for these very reasons.

There are powers that be that stifle evolution in order to maintain the status quo. **The very reason you came to the Earth is for soul evolution, above all else.** It is the will of your soul and the will of GOD that you evolve. This includes your relationships as well. The Higher Consciousness and Energy, which is in

> *The very reason you came to the Earth is for soul evolution.*

alignment with the Universal Principles and the Laws of Creation, will prevail, and is that which is truly real and everlasting.

So when the enslavers tell you that you have to conform and be realistic, they are the ones living the illusion in an unreal world on the edge of collapse. People lack the wisdom, courage and integrity to break the spell of the enslavers and live according to the spirit within. If you were to look in truth at the whole picture, many would either go mad or have nothing for which to live.

Two things happen with enlightenment. When we say enlightenment, we are not talking about those who can only see one side of the coin, living in denial or spiritual ego. We are talking about those who can see it all, the big picture; those who can see how enslaved you truly are.

It would be good to ask yourself how free you are. Are you free to pick up and go in a moment? What if you woke up one day to your soul purpose and found it had nothing to do with your present job, your relationship, your present location? Would you have the courage and detachment to do whatever was necessary to fulfill your soul purpose? Would you fall back into denial and assimilate back into the herd, the status quo?

> *Ask yourself how free you are.*

What if suddenly your eyes were opened, and you realized what you were doing had nothing to do with serving Humanity and Nature, but in truth was serving big business and perpetuating a dependency at the expense of Humanity and Nature? Would you give up your job, your title and position, and change course in a direction that truly serves Humanity and Nature? Would you do it even if it meant losing a lifestyle and all you have gained up to the present? Do your lifestyle and your material acquisitions own you, or do you own them?

If it came to making a choice between the pain, suffering or loss of another, or your job, your lifestyle and your material acquisitions, which would you choose? You have that choice put before you daily. Most close their eyes and their hearts and go on with business as usual in denial, knowing full well within their souls that what they are doing is causing pain, loss or suffering to another or to the environment.

Remember the free energy, the devices that would end most disease, the uneven dispersal of wealth? **Are you part of the problem or part of the solution?** Does your job depend upon war, or the pollution and destruction of your environment? Do you work for a government run by special interests and the international bankers, who support the manufactured lack and create taxes most people work seven months out of the year to pay? If the government owns you seven months out of the year, at what point does it become slavery?

Do your job and your position depend on what can only be called legalized extortion of the people? Is even this message a threat to your survival and security? *If you really think you are free, try not paying your taxes. All of these questions are going to nag you in the days to come. You are going to see just how enslaved, dependent and in denial you are in every part of your life.*

There is a wonderful light which is coming forward within everyone. You might call it the light of honesty, integrity, brotherly/sisterly love, a Higher Consciousness and Energy, a call for equality, individual freedom and prosperity for all. You might even call it the light of truth, which will put an end to denial, loss of individual freedom, lack and all actions against Humanity and Nature! It is a light that is going to enlighten and empower the individual from within.

Telepathy and direct knowing are also by-products of this light. The spell is going to be broken. Everything and everyone is going to be seen for who and what they are. Denial, control, manipulation and the enslavers will be exposed.

You can be part of the solution or part of the problem. Those who choose to be part of the solution will evolve very rapidly, and the love and joy that comes with service, true service to Humanity and Nature, will abound within them. Those who choose to continue to control and manipulate in denial, aligning themselves with the status quo as part of the problem, will experience the solution. The solution is the reaction to their actions, despite their denial.

The worst offenders will shake their fists at GOD, Humanity and Nature up to the bitter end, and deny their attitudes, emotions and actions all the way into the void. Even they will be forgiven once they have gained the wisdom from what they and they alone set into motion.

We can choose the upward spiral of evolution or the downward spiral into social, economic and environmental collapse. Those are your real options, and each choice has consequences.

Once your eyes are opened and your engines are running, do yourself and us a favor. Don't turn around, slip into denial and make a U-turn back into the status quo garage, your comfort zone. We open your eyes and start your engines so that you will go somewhere.

These next chapters are going to further open your eyes. As we said before, **to be enlightened is to know the whole truth, not half-truths. It is seeing the shadow side without denial, and defining the problem, that brings the light or solution where it is needed.**

We are going to shed a lot of light in some very dark corners for the sole purpose of enlightenment, forward evolution and preservation of Humanity and the Earth. In going forward, it is wise to look back to where you've been, so as to gain the wisdom from the experience and not repeat it.

In the Name of Religion and Medicine

This next understanding is going to be very disquieting to some, yet it must be given.

There have been many acts done in the name of GOD and country which in truth were done in the name of religion or the lust for power and money. There have been many prophets, saints and sages who had a profound love for GOD, Humanity and Nature. They have brought universal truths and understandings to Humanity, which would bring unity, peace, individual freedom, equality and prosperity to all. They have been done away with, their teachings falsified, and they have been set up to be worshipped as idols by the very ones who did them in. Now others own them and their teachings, or let us say their version.

There have been geniuses who have created devices that would end most diseases by killing viruses and bacteria, and devices that provide free energy to the individual. They too have been done away with, their inventions patented and kept from the masses.

There has been a grand conspiracy, which has been going on for so long people believe it is normal to war over names, images and doctrines as well as live a life of lack and poor health, facing deadly and debilitating diseases. *A society that accepts manufactured lack, with an economy based on false values and a way of life riddled with senseless death and disease, is a very sick society.* A society where over 80% of the wealth is governed by less than 5% of the people is not freedom, nor should it be acceptable. You need to understand how you got this way, and how the 5% got their power and continue to keep it, often at the expense of Humanity and Nature.

We are going to take a little trip through history to clear up the misperceptions of the past concerning actions by individuals and organizations done in the name of GOD, which in truth were done to serve their own self-interest. In *Becoming Gods* [the first book, which has since been retitled *Reunion with Source*], we spoke of the origin of the wrathful God, which in truth was a mentally and technologically evolved, spiritually backward entity.

This same group created devils and demons and a whole host of events to hold Humanity in subservience. In those days it wasn't hard to do, because Humanity on Earth, which once was very spiritually and technologically evolved, had devolved to become very primitive and superstitious, due to cataclysmic events and wars which almost completely destroyed the planet. There was also a mixture of people who were at different stages of evolution living on the Earth.

There were those who evolved here on the Earth naturally, and those who colonized the Earth. Those who colonized the Earth were much further along in their evolution. They were often referred to as the Annunaki or the Nephilim, the definition of both words meaning "those who came from Heaven to Earth." They were referred to by the primitives as The Gods. When they appeared, it was customary to break out your best lamb or calf, put on a feast, and they sat and broke bread with you.

Some guided the destiny of Humanity selflessly, and others had their own vested interests at heart. Their technology far surpassed today's technology, for they were already working with light and had vehicles and communication devices which worked upon light principles. They could appear and disappear.

They also had lasers and other weaponry which fell into the wrong hands of their own people. This was the cause of the great wars in the heavens, and set the natural disasters and cataclysmic events into motion on Earth. This is where the legends of Atlantis and Lemuria, the great upheavals and biblical floods, originated. Your history goes back even further than that with other civilizations, yet we will use this as a starting point to make our point.

Those of you who use the Bible as the historical records of Earth will continue in a very limited understanding, because it covers an infinitesimal part of Earth's history. There are Sumerian and Babylonian texts which go back even further. There are India, Tibet, China and other ancient cultures which have sustained themselves and kept records far beyond the Middle East. They all speak of extraterrestrial visitors, warring Gods and their great and powerful ships which traversed the heavens.

For those of you who need scientific evidence, **there is a large amount of suppressed archeology that did not fit into the science books, which will surface, as all truth does, in your very near future.** There are great stone columns with writing on them 6,000 feet beneath the surface off the coast of Peru. There is another temple underwater off the coast of Bimini, which has also been found.

There have been skeletons of what is termed Cro-Magnon man, which stand erect at six foot six and have a greater brain capacity than modern man. There are skulls found with massive elongated heads which do not fit into the evolutionary scheme of things, unless you read the Sumerian accounts. They have even found skulls on which brain surgery was performed and the subject went on living. These fossils predate primitive man and exist right alongside other primitive species. In other words, the ape, primitive man and modern man all existed at once side by side.

Some of the oldest living organisms have been found crushed by a human footprint which wore shoes millions of years ago. One of the greatest finds is a diode in rock dated millions of years old. Other finds include crystal skulls with movable jaws which are beyond the ability to recreate with today's technology, and jewelry which represents a very advanced culture living alongside of the dinosaurs even before modern man was known to exist.

There is a fossil which is the remains of a horse, yet where the neck of a horse should have been the torso of a man was found. The skeleton was in perfect order to create what was mythically known as a centaur, which was half-man and half-horse. Rather than accept it for what it was, the scientists postulated that a wild animal killed the horse and the man, dragged them together, ate the neck up of the horse, and ate the waist down of the man. The fact that no remains of the horse's head or any other parts of the man were found and the fact that the spine came together perfectly was irrelevant.

Also found are the remains of little people fully grown at three and a half feet tall, which were mythically known as elves. **Your ancient past, often referred to as myth, was in truth history.** Your

Your ancient past, often referred to as myth, was in truth history.

history goes much further back than two or three thousand years, far beyond any scripture. On the Earth alone, it goes back ten and one half billion years. What has been recorded and what has survived great wars and natural disasters, some of which made the planet uninhabitable or barely inhabitable, is a mere blink of an eye.

There will be secret chambers filled with cultural and scientific knowledge as well as the history of ancient civilizations unveiled in your very near future, which will become a shock to the standard curriculum. It won't be suppressed this time, and all the books will have to be rewritten. If left to the orthodox and conservative religions and governing bodies of the standard curriculum, the Earth would still be flat and the center of the universe.

Now that we have stretched your knowledge of ancient history, we will address the more recent events that have shaped your present civilization. **We spoke of those who set themselves up as Gods and ruled through fear and intimidation. This itself has stunted the evolution of Humanity more than anything else.** This was recorded in many ancient books, including your Bible. Ezekiel, one of my former expressions before my ascension, recorded this event.

There are other references throughout the Old Testament concerning the nature of what was referred to as jealous, wrathful Gods. Have you ever asked yourself why an omnipotent being needs your fatted calves, sheep, and your best grains, fruits and vegetables? How about all those wonderful herbs and incenses? Would an omnipresent being need to eat and have shelter from the elements just like you? Wouldn't he command the elements and live off prana like the other angelic orders beneath him? Couldn't he control his own body temperature and appetite? Why would you have to build them such big houses and call them temples? What better way to live a life of luxury than to walk among primitive, superstitious people and tell them you are Gods.

If they were really omnipresent, by punishing you and causing you pain and suffering, wouldn't it be their own pain and suffering? Why would they demand the sacrifice of your children to prove obedience? Why would they in one moment say, "Thou shalt not kill," and in the next have you war upon all who do not believe in their truth? If GOD is truly omnipresent, would not GOD also be the rest of Humanity in all their diversity, and what about Nature? If there are no divisions in GOD and there is no separation in omnipresence, would there not be an inseparable oneness of GOD, Humanity and Nature?

Why did David slay 200 Philistines, cut off their foreskins (penises) and give them to Saul so he could be with his daughter? Why did Lot sleep with his daughters? Why did Absolom have sex with ten of his father's wives on the rooftops in the sight of all Israel, divinely inspired by God? Why did Joshua slay village after village as the Lord God commanded because they did not have the same beliefs? Why did God keep promising large tracts of land, some of which were already inhabited, to one person and tell that person his people were the chosen ones, only to promise the same land again to another? Why are there totally contradictory stories concerning the death of Saul?

Why are there so many complete contradictions and discrepancies in the Bible? Why was nothing recorded until after at least one to two hundred years after the fact, and how credible are stories passed down through generations? In recorded history, the Bible actually came from a condensation of a whole room full of books and has been translated into different languages, edited and altered by kings and religious institutions, and each believes they have the only true edition.

Has anybody ever questioned why there are over 10,000 religions, each with its own names, images and doctrines, which to this day have not brought unity, peace and brother/sisterhood to Humanity, but instead have brought separation, division and war? What has removing GOD from the hearts and minds of all Humanity, despite their diversity and nature, done to Humanity and Nature? Look at the condition of your planet! Has anybody ever asked these questions? They have, and those who did experienced excommunication, chastisement, immense pain, suffering and death, or mysteriously disappeared.

This has continued to this day, which leads us into the next understanding concerning what has been done in the name of GOD, which in truth was done in the name of religion and power. In the first book, *Reunion with Source,* we spoke about the demise of the feminine God, the mother of all life, who honored all life as family born of the one mother. We also spoke of the destruction and desecration of all temples, statues or things which alluded to her presence and the presence of any other teaching or artifact which does not correspond with the church.

Her fall to the warring herdsmen who worshipped the God of thunder, and the crusades as well as the inquisitions, have caused much of the ignorance and separative beliefs concerning GOD, Humanity and Nature. Not enough can be said about this, and it is covered extensively in *Reunion with Source.* The proof of these ancient cultures and their teachings has either been destroyed by order of the church in its crusades or is hidden beneath the Vatican, which contains a vast wealth of ancient history and artifacts which do not correspond with their doctrines and are secretly hidden from most of Humanity. Despite their efforts, truth will surface as it always does, and it will be beyond their ability to stop it.

We wish to move now into more recent history. **Before the union of the church and the medical establishment, there existed what was called the Wiccans.** Each village had its resident Wiccan, who was in most cases a woman. Her duty was to be a midwife, deliver the children, prescribe herbs and medicines, and provide nurturing, counseling and spiritual guidance to the village. There was a closeness to the land, and the village operated as one family.

The churches did not have the capacity to reach all the villages, and the priests usually stayed within the confines of the church, with an occasional visit to a village here and there. This was also true concerning the medical establishment, which had schools and hospitals.

As their power and numbers increased, the doctors and priests began to venture out into the villages. They arrogantly undermined the Wiccans in the villages, rather than working with them. It became a power struggle. The church banned any future services of the Wiccans and condemned the Wiccans as evil and in league with the devil.

The church was also tied very closely to the ruling parties of the times. They controlled the courts, other enforcement agencies of the courts and had the use of the armies at their disposal. This was known as the Dark Ages, and the beginning of the witch hunts.

The witches were for the better part the herbalists, midwives, nurturers and counselors of the villages. They were beaten, tortured and drowned. Their children were burned with glowing hot iron pokers. Their eyes were burned out of their sockets and hot lead was poured down their throats, all to gain a conviction from their parents and to intimidate the rest of the village. All this was done in the name of GOD.

If the village did not go along with the new order, it was burned to the ground, and those who resisted were killed. This is how the base of power was established in the past by the church and the medical establishment.

At the time, the medical establishment was still bleeding people with leeches to get the bad blood out of them. It was a very sad era, and there are many women to this day who are carrying ancient emotional scars from that experience. If you are one of them, you will feel a strong urge to work with herbal remedies and alternative nurturing methods of counseling, and lean towards spirituality involving Nature over religion. You will also be inhibited by the past in reaching your full potential in these areas until these old wounds and traumas are healed. There will be an underlying fear of being persecuted by the orthodox and conservative religious establishments and the mainstream medical establishment with their FDA, which is often a tool in the modern-day witch hunts. They are known for banning well-known herbal remedies, alternative cures and anything which does not support the hospitals and the drug industries. If they did not invent it, cannot govern it or be the financial beneficiary of these cures and remedies, especially the ones that cure rather than create a dependency on their drugs, they ban them and demonize or persecute any who use them.

Many of these remedies exist to this day through underground movements solely by their own merit and healing abilities. Even the mainstream psychologists believe you must be licensed to nurture and use your God-given intuition. It all boils down to stopping anything which threatens their position or their pocketbook.

According to the laws of today, you have to be a licensed minister or doctor to practice counseling or healing. The ones who license you also control what you use and how you practice. There are a few exceptions to this rule, yet the church and the medical establishment remain as the main powers governing your spiritual and medical needs.

Now I want you to reason this. Remember how they established their power base. What was the motivating force or attitude which drove them? Was it the awakening and healing of Humanity and the Earth? Was it individual freedom, independence and empowering individuals to each find the God within themself? Was it the need to control, to dominate and perpetuate a dependency, exploiting Humanity for their own personal gain? Are these establishments governed by healers and saints, or tyrants and businessmen? Look at the core, the power base, and ask yourself how it was established and what are its true motives. You will be in for a shock!

Those who awaken to this and try to change or step out from under the control of these established orders are ridiculed, chastised, persecuted and excommunicated. They lose their positions, have their licenses revoked, are politically or physically assassinated or mysteriously disappear.

There has never been a weapon nor an army powerful enough that could keep the masses enslaved for very long, other than their own minds. For centuries orthodox and conservative religions have conspired with kings and governments, using images of wrathful Gods and tormenting devils to keep Humanity in check through fear and unworthiness. It is the oldest trick in the book.

First you create an image of God separate from Humanity and Nature. You give it a name and an image—the more ominous and wrathful the better—throw in a few devils and demons to control the ones that get out of line, a lot of guilt and unworthiness, and presto—you've just removed the Divinity out of Humanity and Nature.

It is also good to set yourself up as the go-between. It is very important not to give others the same names, images or doctrines, because after all, we have to keep them separated. This allows you to perpetuate separation and division, demonize other people and religions and conquer or war upon them.

The international bankers love and inspire this, because they can loan money and sell arms to both sides. All you have to do is print some money and place a value on it, and in return you get control over the natural and human resources of both sides. So what if a few million die, and the rest continue to experience lack and suffering; you are in control.

This also maintains your power base as protector. Not only are your image and your armies going to protect the masses from the devils, demons and foreign invaders (that the bankers armed and financed), they are also going to protect the masses from those other ungodly heretics and heathens—you know, the other children of God, despite their diversity; the ones who must be saved or punished, because if you don't, God will punish you.

It's all done in brotherly love, of course; after all, they do need saving, and if we have to kill a few in the process, it was God's plan. The only thing they need saving from is the zealots, the ignorant and the tyrants.

Wake up, people! Do you want to go through another 2,000 years of separation, division and war? Look at the condition of your planet. Do you believe that you can continue to believe you are separate from the very platform for life, and continue to war upon it also? You don't have that luxury. There are no divisions in GOD.

There is a unified field of consciousness and energy in which we all exist. Whatever is not done in the highest and best good of Humanity and Nature or done against Humanity and Nature is done to GOD, the one consciousness that encompasses all consciousness on all planes and all dimensions throughout the universe.

There will always be a reaction to one's actions despite the names, images, doctrines and primitive, superstitious and petty beliefs in separation. No matter whose name you do it in—which includes governments as well—**there is a grand reaction to all actions against Humanity and Nature just around the corner, which will affect everyone individually and collectively, regardless of position and stature.** It will be a great equalizer.

Before we go any further with this, we would like to make it very clear that not all doctors and priests, nor all those within the medical and religious organizations, have dubious intentions or lack integrity. There are many wonderful people within these organizations, dedicated to the awakening and healing of Humanity and the Earth.

Their goals and intentions, as well as their priorities and values, are in order. The health and well-being of those they serve come first before accepted standards. They did not get where they are today at the expense of others or by capitalizing on fear, guilt, unworthiness, others' pain and suffering or the images of wrathful Gods and tormenting devils and demons. It was done honestly through serving others, and these people are often walking on thin ice with their supervisors.

Many doctors are not aware of alternative healing and have been taught within the established schools that most of these alternative healing methods are superstitious myths, do not exist, nor do they work. They are also taught that there is a danger in using them or abandoning the drugs and the knife. Very little is taught about the mind/body connection or attitudes and emotions as being the origin of disease, and they scoff at endless documentation concerning miracle healings through prayer and meditation and herbal formulas. They believe they owe it to their patients to steer them away from all alternative healing. It is programmed into their education.

It is time for them to read their Hippocratic Oath and explore every method possible to heal their patients. Integrity demands that they use what works, despite those who have taken a hypocritical oath to serve themselves and not their patients.

Cancer is big money. Next to the petroleum industry, it is the second largest industry. The carcinogens in pesticides, herbicides and other petroleum products, found even in the air we breathe, keep the cancer and health care industries thriving.

Diabetes is big money. Heart surgery is very big money. What if it could all be avoided and healed very simply? Have you ever gone to a children's cancer ward and watched them suffer through the poisonous effects of chemotherapy, which to this day has little or no proof concerning its ability to prolong life? Have you seen their immune system and organs be utterly destroyed, and seen them die, when it is all unnecessary?

What kind of beast would suppress alternative methods which are relatively painless and inexpensive and have proven to be very successful? What kind of consciousness would create dependencies on drugs, many of which have long term debilitating side effects, when a cure is available? What kind of agency would create laws and enforce them upon doctors who used these alternative methods out of compassion for their patients, especially when all standard methods either fail or make things worse?

Who truly governs these agencies? Is it the drug companies, those who provide the equipment for the hospitals, the hospital administrators? Do they all depend upon the big money generated by the enormous cost of terminal and life-threatening disease? Is it wise to depend upon those who profit greatly from terminal and life-threatening diseases to find a cure that will put them out of business? It's over a trillion dollar a year business.

A cure in the medical industry means less profit, especially when it means the end of a dependency on their drugs or making their expensive equipment unnecessary. What are they going to do if they can't scan you, nuke you and probe you? **In truth, the drug industry regulates the standard practices of doctors.** What happens when the doctors do not use the standard drugs and practices dictated by the AMA and the FDA? They lose their insurance and face losing their license. This is how they perpetuate a trillion dollar industry.

What we are saying is, before you put your spiritual and medical trust in the hands of these institutions or make any contributions, do some research. Look at how it was established. What are its true motives, its goals and intentions? What is the success rate? Does it truly serve Humanity or is it self-serving? Does it promote unity, peace, prosperity, health, well-being and individual freedom for everyone?

Where does the bulk of the donations go? Does it lift and empower the individual, honoring each individual as a unique expression of GOD? Is it free of judgment and condemnation, or does it condemn other beliefs and proven alternative methods of healing? Is money the first priority and motivating factor or driving force behind their institution? Are they truly committed to the highest and best good of Humanity and the Earth?

How big is their GOD? Is it omnipresent within all Humanity and Nature? Does it include you as a unique expression of GOD, even if your beliefs are different, or are you a wretched sinner, separate and unworthy of the grace of

GOD? Are other cultures and beliefs allowed and honored as unique expressions of GOD, or are they to be warred upon, demonized, judged and condemned?

What is a holy war, and who are you warring on, other than the sons and daughters of God in all their diversity? Is the love within your organization unconditional, and what are its limits when it comes to judgment, forgiveness and compassion? Is peace, unity, individual freedom and the awakening and healing of Humanity and the Earth FIRST PRIORITY? Would the major religious and medical institutions give up their images, doctrines, wealth, positions and power for world peace, the end of class separation and disease, and work towards a clean, balanced environment? Would you?

Temples do have their place. They are a place of fellowship, a place where brotherly/sisterly love is practiced. Temples are a place of sanctuary from the ills of society, and hopefully a place where the needs of those who are less fortunate are met. **They are a place for people to find the God within, a God of infinite love, compassion, understanding and forgiveness that honors diversity and allows.**

In a time long since past, the ancient temples were used to heal, initiate young masters and preserve ancient wisdom. They maintained a vibration of love, joy and peace. As time went on they were desecrated, and the institutions which took their place have decayed to what has now often become a business based upon intimidation, promoting fear, unworthiness, guilt and separation. Universal love, joy, peace, unity and administering to the needs of the less fortunate took a lesser priority.

Many have removed GOD out of the hearts and minds of Humanity and set God on a throne far out in the ethers. They have created rigid doctrines, and punishments for not following those rigid doctrines, by a wrathful God or the devil. They have taught people to blame or give credit to God or the devil for everything, rather than teach the basic action/reaction principle, as well as the laws of accountability and responsibility and the fact that consciousness creates reality. They promote the erroneous belief that GOD is separate from you, and all life, for that matter. Has anyone ever contemplated OMNIPRESENCE? How can you or the rest of life be separate from OMNIPRESENCE? There is no separation in omnipresence and there are no divisions in GOD. Their image doesn't add up.

Another point to contemplate is why would a loving father torment his children and torture them by tossing them into a burning pit of everlasting fire? If he were truly OMNIPRESENT, would he not be torturing and condemning himself? Wouldn't their pain and suffering be his pain and suffering? Why would he create devils and demons to torment and deceive his children? Was it a mistake somewhere back in creation? Did GOD one day say, "OOPS, I just created hell and a devil; now what do I do?"

The image of a wrathful GOD is a fictitious one, along with the devil and hell. They were misperceptions of the past and were created to enslave the masses through fear and intimidation. **You have had some very powerful visitors in the past. Some served Humanity and others wanted to be served and worshipped.**

> *The image of a wrathful GOD is a fictitious one.*

There is a greater omnipresent GOD, beyond names and images, that created them, to whom they will have to answer. This does not imply by any means that there is not a shadow side of life. This shadow side is created by error thought within the soul. There are malevolent souls. As above, so below.

There are discarnate spirits or lost souls on other planes. They are being turned around and healed as we speak. Many are by-products of ignorant doctrines, condemnations and judgments. They have taken the fear, unworthiness, guilt and ignorance with them in their passing, and are stuck between worlds because of their beliefs and confusion.

There are those walking the Earth with the same consciousness, yet underneath that consciousness is another consciousness called God. They both need reminding, "As above so below," that an unconditionally loving, joyous, powerful manifesting God resides within them. It's time to lay down their fears, unworthiness and guilt, and go forward in grace from this moment on in service to all life. Everything is forgiven, and everything is possible with GOD.

That which has been given concerning the history of religious and medical institutions will again surface. Many of the barbaric practices in the past upon which current practices were established are continuing to this day. This too will be exposed. Everything shall be made known and seen for what it is.

Everyone will have the knowledge and the chance to choose with whom they are going to align. To whom are they going to give their power? What works and what doesn't work? The ones who choose to take responsibility for their own awakening and healing process, as well as the organizations and institutions which inspire this, that are truly dedicated to the awakening and healing process of Humanity and the Earth, will be the ones that remain standing.

If you are confused as to who is who, then unconditional love, joy, peace, unity and individual freedom and prosperity are wonderful tools for discernment. Look at the goals and intentions, as well as the results. The medical establishments must align themselves with the true purpose for which they were created. They were created to serve and heal the people. **Modern medicine is unsurpassed in the ability to diagnose, yet backward in the ability to heal, mainly because there is big money in finding disease and creating a dependency rather than a cure.**

What if the diagnostic abilities of western medicine went hand in hand with alternative healing? This includes a holistic approach to healing, which includes diet, vitamins, minerals, herbal remedies, frequency generators and the mind/body connection. How about process-oriented techniques to clear the attitudes and emotions which are the primary cause of disease?

Quantum physics, enlightened physicians and psychologists agree that there is a matrix of consciousness and energy which is first and foremost to the physical. They believe mental, emotional and physical disorders often exist within this matrix as an unresolved issue or energy imbalance. **The effects of laughter, prayer and meditation in accelerating the healing process are already well documented.**

There is also the transference of subtle energies. **There are vitamin, mineral and herbal remedies which cause the body to heal and balance itself,** which do not just provide symptomatic relief or regulate the disease, creating dependencies on drugs.

There are also suppressed technologies which can eradicate every bacteria and virus known to man and also can eradicate parasites. It can all be done with a mere flick of a switch, without harm to the human cells, which are 10,000 times more resilient than the virus or bacteria cells and the parasites which are specifically targeted. Isn't this a better idea than using barbaric radiation, which destroys the immune system and life-sustaining organs? This is not to mention the other tortuous side effects.

How about the drugs and their poisonous side effects, not to mention the dependencies? Do you know how many people die each year from mixing medications or from wrong prescriptions? The medical institutions and those within them are going to have to make a choice. Will they continue to support a barbaric institution bent upon perpetuating itself at the expense of Humanity, or explore every means necessary to serve and heal Humanity?

Despite whether or not it is accepted by the system as it now stands, which is not very effective in accomplishing its professed goals, are we going to continue to allow profit to be the decisive force in health care, or the health and well-being of Humanity? Those who chose the healing profession took an oath; it is time to have enough integrity to honor that oath.

As for the religious institutions, those within them also took an oath to serve God and Humanity over and above the institution. They too are going to have to make a choice. Will they continue in promoting fear, unworthiness and images of wrathful Gods and tormenting devils in order to control and manipulate, which are the barriers to unification with the Creator? Will they promote love, joy, individual freedom and an image of a loving, joyous, wise and powerful manifesting GOD, an OMNIPRESENT GOD, a GOD that is within all Humanity, Nature and all creation?

GOD is the unified field of consciousness and energy and universal life force that ties and binds all together as one. Why not worship the GOD that created all the prophets, all Humanity and Nature in all its diversity?

Those who choose to promote fear, unworthiness and wrathful images to control and manipulate will have their fill. The fear, guilt and unworthiness will all be amplified and accelerated, and they will be a wretched lot. Their ministries will diminish as people turn to love, joy, unity and individual freedom.

There will be a turning away from religion and a movement towards spirituality. The names, images and doctrines, as well as the need to defend them, will also take a lesser priority to universal principles. The Buddhist, the Christian, the Hindu, the Muslim, the Native American—all faiths will break bread together, and they will find great similarities in the deeds and words of their teachers, prophets and healers. They will transcend religious and cultural barriers.

The divisions will be no more. Those who wish to perpetuate the divisions will be exposed for who they are and what they truly represent, and that is a lust for wealth and power individually and collectively.

There are no divisions in GOD. There is diversity, yet there are no divisions. Whether you be white, red, yellow or black, the life force is the same. Whether you believe in different images and doctrines, the life force that binds all together still remains the same. What befalls the beast and the forest befalls man. A selfish, inconsiderate act against life, no matter what form it takes, be it Humanity or Nature, is a selfish, inconsiderate act against GOD.

It takes life to sustain life. This understanding is by no means to create guilt or condemn any who partake of the animal kingdom to sustain self. **It is how one partakes of life that determines one's life.**

For an animal to give its life to sustain Humanity is an honor and a service. It is a gift that must be honored. It is not man against the beast. It is not the conquest of the fish, fowl or beast for ego gratification. It is not the overpowering nor the outsmarting of the game that truly brings satisfaction to the soul and sustenance to the body. **It is gratitude for what was given and a strong reverence for life that feeds the body.**

The same goes for the tree, the fruits, the vegetables, the grains, etc. Bless and give thanks to the tree that gave you the lumber to build your house. Bless and give thanks to the tree that gave you fruit, the plants that gave you the vegetables, the fields that gave you grain and the vines that gave you the berries. Give thanks to the herb that seasoned your food and healed your body. Know that when you are consuming them you are consuming a gift from God, the gift of life to sustain life. Bless and give thanks to all that you eat and all who grew and prepared it. Do it with feeling. Don't make an empty ritual out of it.

When you go to bed at night, pray for the white man, the red man, the black man and the yellow man. Pray that the divisions, the wounds and traumas of the past, and the prejudices all be healed and done away with. Pray for peace, unity and the knowledge that despite the diversities, the life force that binds every living thing is shared and given from the same source, regardless of names and images. Pray that each individual be honored as a unique expression of GOD, and that a strong reverence for life and gratitude for the gift of life resound in the hearts and minds of all Humanity.

It only takes a few to change the destiny of a nation.

Step out of the past and choose a different path. Choose a path of love, honesty and integrity in service to Humanity and Nature which honors the sacred circle of life, the path home.

The Life of Jesus, BC

In order to truly understand the life and purpose of Jesus, we must first go back even further in time before his advent upon the Earth. This will bring a greater understanding to his mission, why it was necessary and who he parlayed with in the wilderness and the mountaintops.

We spoke earlier concerning the fall of man from spirit as he lowered himself into the body and got caught in the lower vibrational attitudes and emotions that came with the physical. **It was the desire of the Creator Gods to experience that which they created. To do so they needed a physical body within this dimension, equipped with the five senses.**

In order for a higher vibrational being to experience a lower vibration, they must lower their vibration and inhabit a body. To truly experience the physical, one must become the physical, or one would not be able to touch, feel, smell, hear or taste the physical world. They could see the physical, feel its vibration and know its thought emanations, yet could not truly embrace it without becoming it.

Existing within the material universe are civilizations which have been going on for billions of years in other parts of the universe. There are other third dimensional worlds inhabited by very advanced civilizations. Some of these civilizations have even gone on to evolve into other dimensions and have energy or light bodies. These beings are expressing more and more the nature of God and have greater knowledge and command over the creational energies which flow through all life. There is an ancient saying, **"The more one knows and understands the nature of GOD, the more one becomes GOD."**

Each planet where the conditions are conducive to life has in its course of evolution its race of Humanity. Their bodies are physical adaptations to their environments. **The Earth is very unique because it has its own race of Humanity, along with several other races which colonized the Earth.** The first of these colonies came from Lyra millions of years ago. They were a very tall race (up to 30 feet) of white-skinned people with a long history of war and the conquering of other planets and civilizations. They had a history of building grand civilizations, only to destroy themselves in power struggles, not only from within but from without by other warring factions of their own people.

The first colonies were a failure, because not only did they destroy themselves, the home planet also underwent great wars of incredible destruction, and their final destruction came from the heavens when a great destroyer comet paid a visit to their home world.

Many peaceful Lyrians, tired of the wars and power struggles, fled the home world to colonize other systems. They settled into the Pleiades, Orion and the Haydes systems. Thousands of years of evolution passed, and their bodies adapted to the size of the planets they inhabited and are much like us, only a little taller. **They continued to evolve, had their wars, and eventually, after thousands of years of peace, from there they tried another attempt to colonize Earth.**

This will bring a new understanding to Genesis, chapter 6, which reads, *"And it came to pass when the men began to multiply on the face of the Earth, and daughters were born unto them, that the sons of God saw the daughters of men that they were fair; and they took to them wives of all which they chose."* This was the second coming of the peaceful Lyrians, who were now called Pleiadians. Genesis, chapter 6, verse 4, reads, *"There were giants in the Earth in those days; and also after that when the sons of God came in unto the daughters of men, and they bore children to them, the same became the mighty men which were of old, men of renown."*

The giants were the remnants of the old Lyrians. The Pleiadians found that the original Lyrian colonies which began roughly 450,000 years ago had degenerated and become very primitive because of the great wars which destroyed their technology. The Earth also underwent natural disasters in which civilization further degenerated into base survival.

They were shocked to see some of the experimentation which occurred concerning combining the genetics of man with animals. These experiments went on for hundreds of years and are recorded in your ancient history. Many of the mythological creatures, including half-man half-animal, did exist as a result of this experimentation. The horse and the goat are ancestors of the mythological unicorn. There was a half-man and half-goat, half-man and half-horse, and several other varieties that were experimented with in order to create an intelligent beast of burden and for the mere sake of scientific accomplishment. There are fossils which have been found that testify to this, yet your scientists deny their authenticity.

This same technology exists today, and scientists can now clone and alter species. Most of these creations were hybrids and could not reproduce; therefore they died and did not continue as a species, and those which did survive were killed. **It is the nature of man to fear and destroy that which he doesn't understand or which is different.**

There was also what was termed primitive ape-man and ape-woman, who were also experimented upon. **Another scientist, wanting to undo the acts of his forefathers, later decided to create another form of Humanity.** He and his followers added their seed again, creating a hybrid, which is the reason for the missing link and the quantum leap in man's evolution. **This time they further genetically adapted the hybrid to reproduce. This was the first Adam.**

The previous upheavals and wars 50,000 years ago destroyed most of the life forms on the planet, and the seed of Adam and his wife Eve were to be the next form of man to inhabit the Earth. It was the seed of Adam and a mixing of seed over thousands of years that the returning Pleiadians found to be the fair daughters of men referred to in the Bible. The ape-man/woman, if left alone, would have evolved in the natural course of evolution to what is now known as modern man through creative evolution—it would have just taken longer. The first jump in evolution was to serve the Lyrians, who in ancient terms were described as the Anunnaki or Nephilim; the second jump was done selflessly to undo the sins of the past, and it was done in a place called Eden.

The Earth was not the only planet where the creation game was occurring. There were three planets in a cradle orbit around your Sun. One was Melona, another was Mars and the third was Earth. Melona was much larger than Earth, and the Lyrians first began their colonization within this solar system on Melona. Over time they began to compete with each other in power struggles, and the competition became so fierce the entire planet was blown to bits. The remnants of Melona make up your asteroid belt and account for many of the meteors and falling stars.

> *Earth was not the only planet where the creation game was occurring.*

The Lyrians learned a great lesson from Melona; many went off to distant galaxies to begin anew, and some remained. Mars was also in a cradle orbit and inhabited by the same group. The destruction of Melona blew Mars out of its cradle orbit, destroying that civilization as well. The remnants of this civilization can still be seen as stone pyramids, monuments and great canals which once brought water from the poles to the equator. The Earth was spared the destruction of Melona and Mars, and was moving along in its evolutionary process.

The Creator Gods of Earth, often referred to as the Constants, had learned valuable lessons from Melona and

Mars. They decided to install within their creation what you would term a fail-safe system. It would trigger if the consciousness of Earth fell to the level where it would destroy itself. This mechanism is built into Nature herself and into Humanity as well. The Earth is known as the action/reaction world, or the plane of demonstration where consciousness creates reality. The words, "As you believe, so it is," and "As you sow, so shall you reap," refer to this. This check and balance system is often referred to as karma, or the action/reaction principle. It was created to ensure the continuation of evolution of the Earth and its peoples.

The Creator Gods of Earth did not want Earth to succumb to the same path of Melona and Mars. They wanted to ensure that Earth evolved and did not devolve into competition, war, greed and decadence. Those who chose this path eventually created their own demise, yet the Earth would not be completely destroyed and would regenerate after each collective lesson. Your present civilization is the fourth grand cycle, or world, as the ancient prophecies refer to it, and you are entering the fifth.

The Constants wanted the physical to evolve to its greatest heights, and love, joy, peace and brother/sisterhood to reign supreme. The evolution of Earth was spiral in nature. It often seemed as if they were going around in circles, yet evolution was going forward. Civilizations came and went, learned their lessons, and those who were of a warlike, competitive nature did themselves in at their own hand.

There were many civilizations which rose to a very advanced stage, left monuments as testimonies to their existence, and ascended into another time flow or took up residence elsewhere. There were civilizations which, due to their technology evolving greater than their spirituality, did themselves in or fell to the reaction of Nature's cataclysms due to their lust for power and their unbridled greed.

The Earth is over ten billion years old, and there have been many civilizations that have come and gone within that time frame. Your scientists have found relics of advanced civilizations existing right alongside your dinosaurs. Of course, they can't release this or certify it as authentic, because it upsets their theories and standard beliefs, primitive as they may be.

One thing your scientists have not realized is that their dating methods based on the Sun's radiation of an object are off, because the Earth existed for four billion years shrouded in a dense cloud cover which the Sun did not penetrate. There are new dating methods which are constantly pushing back time, and archeological finds which are turning history upside down.

Many historians cannot fathom the complete destruction of civilizations due to powerful wars and natural cataclysms which shifted continents, causing them to rise and fall and oceans to reel across the surface, forcing the survivors to start over as primitives. Many cannot even fathom the Earth's history going back ten billion years.

> *Many historians cannot fathom the complete destruction of civilizations.*

Some believe evolution started 3,000 to 4,000 years ago because their sacred book tells them so, which is a blink of an eye in Earth's history. Some religions still believe the Earth is the center of the universe and where life began. Your scientists have dated Earth back four or five billion years, depending on whose theory you accept, yet that will change as the new dating methods come forward. What do you think is going to happen when they realize there are other civilizations, galaxies and whole universes, along with other planes and dimensions, which have evolved billions upon billions of years in the time flow before Earth began?

Now that we have expanded your reference points and your reality concerning the history of Earth and the vastness of the universe along with the infiniteness of creation, we can continue with a small part of your history which is misunderstood and misrecorded. We will begin just previous to the cataclysms of Atlantis and Lemuria, or Mu, as some refer to it.

Atlantis and Lemuria were very advanced civilizations, which were technologically superior to your own. They were colonies consisting of civilizations which came from the stars. They began with the second attempt by the peaceful Lyrians from the Pleiades to once again colonize the Earth.

There was another race of primitive people naturally evolving on the Earth existing right alongside of the colonies. These new colonists, rather than experiment with Humanity or bond them into slavery, treated them kindly, with respect. There was a mixing of their genetics with the already existing races, resulting in another quantum leap in evolution.

Many of the people who came to the colonies were fleeing from great wars in other galaxies. Some were merely pioneers and seekers of peace. They began two colonies: one named Atlantis and the other Mu, often referred to as Lemuria. They lived for thousands of years in peace, and this attracted others from the stars, who began to set up their own colonies.

There was the black-skinned race from Sirius, the yellow race from the Orion system, the brown race, which were the ones evolving naturally on the Earth, and several in-betweens, due to the mixing of genetics. Things went very smoothly until the scientists and several leaders again fell into their old ways of war, dissension and lust for power. Mistrust between the two great civilizations of Atlantis and Mu continued to escalate, and they completely destroyed each other in a war so devastating it triggered the natural cataclysms. Lemuria was melted to the ground by the fleet of Atlantis as they took to the sky in their great ships with lasers of intense heat and destruction. Almost all traces of Lemuria were wiped clean from the Earth.

There were Lemurian scientists deep in space who had the technology to guide comets and meteors. They guided one such meteor to target Atlantis, and the meteor exploded just above it with a blast and heat so severe that Atlantis was erased from the face of the Earth in moments. The impact of the meteor hit with an incredible force so strong it knocked Earth off its axis to its present rotation. The wars and natural cataclysms were so great that they erased all but a very few remnants of two once-great civilizations, burying them under ash, oceans or beneath the ice. It was a tremendous leap backward in evolution, because the few remaining survivors 10,500 years ago had to start over as primitives.

For years the Earth was almost completely uninhabitable. It was as if all history had been erased. Those few survivors who remained had gone from a very advanced civilization again back to base survival. They began to rebuild with the resources at hand, which were very limited, and it took thousands of years for the Earth to heal.

> *For years the Earth was almost completely uninhabitable.*

During that time, the rest of the universe settled down and the other galaxies evolved (all but a few) beyond war. When one such group from the Pleiades returned to Earth, they were again shocked by the condition of Earth and the demise of the colonies. They found, however, the primitive culture to be very beautiful; and the Earth, though rearranged a bit since their last visit, was also very beautiful.

The remaining colonists tried to preserve their consciousness by creating stories which reminded them of the past and their true heritage, which was from the stars. Many of these stories continue to be told as legends and myths of the Star Nations. Very few realize the importance of these legends and myths, as well as the truth within them. They are seen as far-fetched, unrealistic and blasphemous in some religious understandings, which have gone out of their way to destroy any physical evidence pertaining to the truth of these legends and myths. Nonetheless, proof is continuously surfacing globally for those with inquiring minds.

The Pleiadians who came to Earth decided to leave Earth alone and allow it to evolve on its own. Those who were once great warriors, great scientists and great in their understanding of universal energies had degenerated again in consciousness over thousands of years. Nothing remained of their powerful ships, and their technology was also long forgotten.

One of their enemies, a great and powerful warrior named Jehovah, whom they had defeated earlier in ancient battles, came to the Earth, only to find that his enemy had degenerated into a very superstitious, fearful adversary that was easy to control. They had no ships to confront him, and those who retained their consciousness and their memories were few.

He decided to set himself up as God and punish the remaining Pleiadians for his earlier defeat. His anger, wrath and punishment were beyond measure, and it is recorded in your religious texts. He was the jealous, wrathful God who would have no Gods before him. He erected armies out of primitive superstitious men. He created the Ark of the Covenant, which was a powerful weapon of immense destruction that if anyone touched (except for the Nubians, who were immune to its radiation) they would die an instant death.

The Nubians would march with the Ark into battle, and anyone in front of its path would experience unmerciful pain and destruction. Their insides would explode, their flesh would melt away, and those who didn't die instantly wished they would have.

Jehovah also flew his great ships with weapons of immense destruction against primitive people with spears, swords and shields. **His wrath lasted hundreds of years.** Entire cities were destroyed for not bending to his desires and worshipping him as the only sovereign God of Earth.

A great cry went out into the heavens and was heard

by a peaceful people who hated war and all resemblances of war. They took council and sent a message through the prophets of Earth that there would come a great one from the heavens who will bruise the head of the one who bruised the head of man.

The Pleiadians, after their last encounter defeating Jehovah and during his wrath upon Earth, experienced thousands of years of peace. They evolved very rapidly in their technology and their knowledge concerning the creational energies. Jehovah had not evolved, because he sought only power. He could not go further in evolution, because the next level of consciousness was love, and it meant giving up the desire to rule and overpower others. Love always empowers and serves Humanity, and **Jehovah's only desire was to overpower and be served. This attitude is expressed to this day in a grand misperception concerning GOD throughout many religious institutions.**

In the Pleadians' desire for peace and to experience more love, joy and compassion in their lives serving Humanity and Nature, they evolved to a much higher level of consciousness on their home planet. With this higher evolution in consciousness came a rise in their vibration as a collective, and they entered a new time. Their spirituality and technology also took a quantum leap, and they advanced very rapidly, far beyond anything Jehovah could imagine. They also had come in contact with other spiritually advanced beings who had evolved far beyond them in consciousness, with even a greater command over the creational energies.

The Pleiadians took council with a group of beings in a distant universe which were beyond the need for a material body, because they had transcended beyond the need for one. Their wisdom, love and power concerning the use of the creational energies far transcended their own, and **one of them felt a great compassion for the people of Earth and decided to incarnate upon the Earth as a prophet and a healer.**

The Pleiadians returned to Earth with a great prophet and healer and a force that was beyond anything Jehovah had ever seen. His ships were no match for their ships of immense light, power and speed. His army was defeated down to just a few surviving ships, and **Jehovah fled to a far off distant galaxy, never to return.**

There was a great overlord of immense beauty known as Yahweh, the God of love and peace. There were also 12 Grand Masters who were overseers concerning the evolution of Earth. They held council with the new prophet and healer, transferring all of their knowledge and talents in preparation for his mission.

Plans had already been underway for the advent of the prophet to take up residence upon the Earth and begin his mission. There was a complication concerning the physical body he was to inhabit, because his consciousness and energy was far too great, and a special body was needed to utilize the full expression of his spirit. **A woman of Lyrian descent was chosen and she was impregnated by a very advanced and genetically superior being by the name of Gabriel.** It was referred to as an immaculate conception. The woman's name was Mary, and she was raised by the Essenes.

Joseph, who was to be her husband, was very disturbed upon the realization that Mary was with child, and was undecided as to wed, due to her unfaithfulness. He was contacted in a dream and was told that the child was a great prophet born of immaculate conception and that Mary had been true to him. He was told to marry her and raise the child as his own for the good of all Humanity. He was also told that he would be guided when and where to go and to not hesitate upon receiving guidance, but to act. There was a great ship seen as a star in the heavens that guided other wise and gifted men to pay homage to the prophet that would fulfill the prophecies of old.

Thus was born, to Mary and Joseph, Yeshua Ben Joseph, who was later to be called Jmmanuel, or Jesus. He spoke of a God whose love, forgiveness and compassion were beyond measure. His prayer was, "Beloved Father, let them be one, as we are one." He spoke of other flocks diverse in culture and belief, and spoke of a time when man will neither worship God in the temples nor in the mountains, but within self. He also gave another prophecy, which has been fulfilled: "My teachings will be falsified and twisted by scribes and Pharisees, millions will die in my name, and only after 2,000 years will man awaken to their true message." That time is fast approaching.

His message was one of love, forgiveness, peace and unity. The worshipping and defending of names, images and doctrines which cause separation, division and war were never his intentions.

Those who continue to perpetuate the myths of wrathful Gods and punishing devils to intimidate the masses, promoting fear, unworthiness and guilt, are working in ignorance or for their own self-aggrandizement and lust for power and wealth. This will be seen clearly in the days to come.

Humanity will find the God of love, joy, power and wisdom, the God of peace. The temple is within. **Celebrate the God within each individual, within all life, and be one with all people and all life. Then you will see the face of GOD, diverse as it may be.**

The Last Prayer of Jesus

"Beloved Father, do you think they understood the true meaning of my message, my life? That Ye are all Gods, and that Ye will do greater works than I, for I am leaving this plane. Do you think they understood my prayer when I said, 'Beloved Father, let them be one as we are one,' that within them resides a loving, joyous, wise and powerful manifesting God waiting to unfold? Do you think they understood the true meaning of my death and my resurrection, which was to conquer the greatest of all challenges and fears, which is death itself? Do you think they understood unconditional love, infinite compassion and forgiveness? Will it take another 2,000 years of fear, unworthiness, separation and the worshipping and warring over names, images and doctrines before they find peace, unity and the God within them? Will they ever understand the one law which supersedes all laws, which is the Law of Love?"

A Fantasy Called Death

During the vibrational lifting and healing process, many will be exalted to great heights of love, joy, health and well-being. There will be others that will not fare so well. Their unresolved issues and reactions to their actions, followed by the corresponding diseases, will overcome them.

There are also those who have finished their business upon this plane and choose to leave. It is all in order; and because so many are going to make their transition, it is of the utmost importance to address the issue of transition, or death, as so many refer to it.

Nothing ever dies. The life force always continues, yet there is a transition. The life force is in the atom, and the body only begins a process of disassembling itself after the spirit leaves the body. This is often referred to as the process of decomposition, where the vehicle or body begins disassembling itself from a complex organism back to the elements, which break down further back to the atomic structure.

The spirit or soul moves on to another adventure, often later to start the process all over again. In the process of reassembling, the atoms to create the molecules come together, forming more complex structures until an even more complex structure known as the body begins to take shape.

The spirit, or soul substance, as it is referred to by your scientists, has weight. Experiments have measured a loss of weight at the exact time of death, for which there is no conventional accounting. The excretion of fluids remains on the bed and can be weighed, evaporation cannot account for the loss of weight, and filling the lungs with air again also cannot make up for it. The loss of weight is the removal of the remaining soul substance from the body. Before death the soul begins removing itself from the body, and often leaves enough soul substance to maintain or keep the body alive until it is comfortable with its new existence on another plane or to take care of unfinished business on this one.

When a person slips into a coma, they have left the body and are making a decision whether to return or move on. They have left just enough of their soul substance or consciousness to maintain the body. They can remove it and let the body expire, or return. Those who return are never the same, and it is an adjustment for all concerned.

Those on Earth, for those who wish to reincarnate, maintain the ongoing life support system that allows all this to take place. **It is not uncommon, and most often the case, that the spirit returns to the same family or lineage from which it left.**

Only the spirit decides where it chooses to incarnate, and it is not limited to this plane and dimension, or the lineage it left behind. There are other planes and dimensions with civilizations that have existed billions of years in the time flow, where some return after their Earth experience.

Many have come to the Earth as missionaries to help Earth to evolve, and some are here for their own evolution. There are infinite possibilities concerning where one goes after their transition. The main thing that determines where you go after your transition is your consciousness. One cannot enter the higher planes and dimensions unless there is love in his or her heart, and the consciousness to match.

The majority of people after their transition move through what is known as the tunnel opening into the spirit world. There they are met by friends and family or guides, depending upon their evolution. There is an adjustment period which also depends upon how they made their transition and the condition of their consciousness or soul. Those who have had a very traumatic life or died a sudden or painful death often have a longer adjustment period than others.

There are some who don't even make it into the heavens, or what is referred to as the light. These are often referred to as ghosts or wayward spirits, which are caught between worlds because of extreme trauma, attachment, unfinished business and refusal to accept help or go through the tunnel into the world of spirit.

There are mental planes where whatever a spirit thinks manifests very swiftly. The lessons come much quicker there than on the Earth because the action/reaction principle is accelerated, along with the manifestation process. Consciousness creates reality on these planes as well, only at a much faster pace. They have a body which is physical to that vibration, and everything on that vibration is physical to them, yet to this level they would be seen as an energy or light principle.

Many people experience a reunion of loved ones who have made their transition, feeling their presence or seeing them clairvoyantly. They may appear in order to tell them they are all right, take care of some unfinished business, or may come in need of a healing.

The astral levels consist of many levels of consciousness, the lowest of which is filled with malevolent, confused spirits of a very low vibrational nature. As one moves out of the gray astral levels and into the light, there is less confusion, less suffering, and the souls there are taking more responsibility for their attitudes, emotions and the world they are manifesting. The mid-levels are where most people go and often continue business as usual, yet they too have experienced a quickening and will often be perceived differently because they are now more loving and understanding.

After their transition, the majority of people often reach the same conclusions concerning their lives on Earth. When asked if they could do it all over again, what would they do, they often reply, "I would have loved more, forgiven more and would not have taken life so seriously."

They also wish they could have been of more service in some way to Humanity and the Earth. It is not uncommon for them to remember some of their last thoughts upon the

Earth—how they wished they could have resolved the unfinished business between friends, family and lovers through forgiveness. They look around at all their possessions, and how much time and energy was spent acquiring them. They look at the time spent away from loved ones and doing what truly brought them joy, and realize they will never be able to recapture that time.

They also realize that they cannot take any of their material acquisitions with them. The only thing they can take with them is their consciousness, how they feel about themselves, the way they treated others, their actions either for or against Humanity and Nature, and the wisdom they have acquired. All this determines where they go in their next understanding. **They realize their main purpose in coming to the Earth was to evolve the soul into higher states of love, joy, compassion and wisdom and to be a blessing to life.**

The journey after their transition begins with a grand review of just how well they did. Rather than judgment day, we would rather it be referred to as review day, because it is not done with judgment or condemnation. It is done for the good of the soul, so it can do things a little better on the next go-around.

The Guides and Masters assist souls in their decision as to where and when they will reincarnate and what would best serve them to evolve the soul, yet they never make that decision. Free will is honored above and below, yet souls see the wisdom in their advice and make the right decision.

A helpful hint concerning your future is not to do anything you would be ashamed of facing later in the company of an Angelic Guide or Ascended Master. Why? Because nothing is hidden in Spirit. The higher levels consist of increasingly higher states of love, joy and wisdom. There are many teachers and healers existing on these levels, yet they are still on the wheel of reincarnation. Though noble in their virtue, they are held back by their own consciousness, often due to their beliefs; still having a little fear, unworthiness or religious or superstitious dogma to release. They have not yet mastered judgment or the false belief of separation.

As one transcends the last of their misperceptions, they ascend beyond the astral levels into the Christ Consciousness and beyond. They are now off the wheel of reincarnation and only return by choice to help Humanity. In times of great transition they come to assist Humanity to get through tumultuous times and continue in their evolution.

Presently Earth is on the edge of a great transition, and there are many Grand Masters who are both incarnate and in the process of reincarnating. It is as if all the prophets of the past are coming forward, seen and unseen, to see the culmination of their work over many lives. These enlightened ones are drawing to Earth an even greater consciousness, along with other spiritually and technologically advanced beings, to aid in the awakening and healing process. **Those who cannot make it through the awakening and healing process in their physical embodiments will continue their education within the levels of spirit.** They may even return in spirit to help loved ones back on Earth, reincarnate again through those loved ones, or go off on another adventure somewhere else.

> *Earth is on the edge of a great transition.*

Life is continuous. Although you have a body and a personality, beyond that lies all of creation, with infinite possibilities. The only limits are set by you and your consciousness.

There are many questions as to what to do when a loved one passes this plane. **You can be of immense help to a soul both during and after his or her transition.** It is very important that he or she has a chance to resolve any unfinished business with friends, family, lovers or whatever else comes up. There will be Angelic Guides and Ascended Masters to help orchestrate this. Follow your feelings in this regard, for you also will be guided concerning your part to play. Do not take responsibility for the outcome.

Inspire each individual to find the courage to forgive and to resolve any issues while there is still time. Assure the individuals making their transition that everything will be all right. Release them by telling them you support their decision if they choose to make their transition. Tell them all is forgiven, and there will be loved ones waiting just on the other side to help them in their transition. Advise them to focus on as much love, joy and forgiveness as possible, and try to release any fear and unworthiness. This helps those on the other side to connect with them.

Call upon their own Higher Selves or your own Angelic Guide or Ascended Master to help them in their transition. Most importantly, realize that some things are beyond your control and are in greater hands than yours. Release the outcome to those greater hands, knowing there is purposeful good, no matter what happens. **Even death can be a healing and necessary part of an individual's soul evolution.**

The only tragedy in death is when nothing was learned from the experience. When one makes his or her transition, it leaves behind a great impact on everyone. **Many realize through the death of another that they themselves have forgotten to live.** There are many lessons left behind. When reflecting upon the life of another who has made his transition, they see the things they loved about him, as well as the things they didn't love. They see the accomplishments and the mistakes he made. Hopefully, they can be inspired by his accomplishments and learn from his mistakes, and not make the same mistakes themselves.

There are many phases people go through after the tran-

Many realize through the death of another that they themselves have forgotten to live.

sition of a loved one. There is often denial, grief, loneliness and sadness, and there are those who cannot overcome their grief because of their own misperceptions concerning death, or a great dependency.

There are some that have a lot of unspoken feelings who believe that if they speak them now they will go unheard. They do not realize that **the mere thought of an individual after their transition puts them in contact with them,** and everything can still be said.

There are those who realize death is only a transition, a necessary part of life before the beginning of a new life, and they grieve very little, but sometimes judge themselves for not grieving. They feel guilty because a sense of relief has come upon them, and God forbid, they may even be happy. They may even try to hide their happiness so as not to be judged as cold and unfeeling. To be happy for a soul that has made his or her transition is not cold and unfeeling; it is only a sign of a greater awareness. Why do Angels sing when one makes his or her transition? Because it is a birth into the heavens.

It is important to grieve, and not stuff or deny your feelings. One has to finish saying good-bye before he or she can say hello. **It is very important to release loved ones who have made their transition, severing all bonds, and send them as much love and joy as possible to assist them in reaching the higher planes of consciousness.**

Loved ones are often waiting for those they left behind to finish grieving, before they can ascend to higher levels. Until they are finished grieving, they cannot contact them to let them know they are all right and everything is well, because the grief, sadness and belief that they are spiritually gone creates a dense wall of consciousness they cannot penetrate, blocking any further communication.

The contacts often come in dreams and feelings of their presence, when a person is ready. Many people are contacted just before sleep or in between the waking and sleeping state. It is important to realize that while most contacts are beneficial, there are some contacts that are not. A wonderful saying is, **"Just because you are dead does not mean you are enlightened."**

There are a lot of spirits on the astral level that are not much smarter than when they left Earth. There are some very malevolent and confused spirits that didn't go anywhere. They are referred to as wayward spirits or lost souls. They are very close to the physical and are often referred to as ghosts or poltergeists, who are often deceased children. That is why they play so many pranks.

They are often riddled with lower vibrational attitudes and emotions, such as fear, anger and jealousy, or suffered great pain in their transition. Some had a lot of unfinished business, keeping them Earth-bound. They can and are healed frequently, very easily, we might add, with the help of the Angelic Guides and Masters, unless one desires to make a movie. Then, of course, it is wise to keep them around for a while longer.

There will be a lot of this activity in this arena, because Humanity is becoming more sensitive and aware of other planes and dimensions due to the vibrational lifting process. With this greater sensitivity and awareness comes an adventure into new territory, a greater consciousness. Along with the expanded consciousness comes a greater responsibility to heal what is within it. This was referred to extensively in the first book, *Reunion with Source* [which was originally titled *Becoming Gods*], and the tools and techniques were again given in the present book on page 31.

In conclusion, we live in a world of infinite possibilities. **What determines where one goes after one's transition is determined by his or her consciousness.** Those who are very loving, joyous, have been a blessing to life and who have the knowledge and awareness of the higher planes and dimensions will gain access to them. No one enters the higher planes and dimensions unless they have love in their heart. Love is the key.

The higher planes and dimensions are only more ex-

panded states of pure, unconditional love and joy. Commit to serving life, be it Humanity or Nature, for GOD is omnipresent within all life. Behave as if the God in all life matters. Do nothing of which you would be ashamed. Behave as if an Angel was on your shoulder, for there will come a day when everything will be reviewed alongside an Angel. Forgiveness is also infinite, and there is no better day than today to begin anew.

It is by your choice that you change, and both the doing and the undoing will be by your hand. All that is eternal and everlasting is consciousness. It creates your tomorrow and determines your next understanding after your transition.

It's never too late to heal or change. There is an entity of immense beauty, unfathomable love and joy which is patiently waiting to emerge from within each and every one of you. It is the unfolding of the true self beyond the personality, the light principle within you, beyond all your woes and misperceptions. There is a loving, joyous, wise and powerful manifesting God within everyone, a potential waiting to unfold that only has to be realized and accepted to come forward.

Dreams, Visitations, Visions and Interdimensional Mind

This next dissertation is concerning some of the byproducts of Higher Consciousness and Energy.

Dreams will become very important in the days to come. There are many types of dreams, and it is very important to understand what type of dream you have had before trying to interpret the dream.

There are processing dreams, which are literal or symbolic for the purposes of healing, releasing and gaining the wisdom from past experiences, including past lives. **There are prophetic dreams,** which warn or inform an individual of future experiences. Some of these dreams are often based

---

upon the present mental states of those concerned and current outer appearances, which can be altered at any time; others concern events which are on the books, so to speak, which will occur in the future.

There are dreams which are inspired by the Beautiful Many Saints, Sages and Ascended Masters, as well as your own Higher Selves in their inspirational and healing endeavors. There are dreams that are inspired by lower astral beings, which are often filled with fear, judgment and opposition. This includes nightmares or dreams which may leave you feeling somewhat sick, sad or uncomfortable in the morning.

Some dreams are just downloading the events of the day, or concern what you were focused upon when you went to bed. **There are also dreams which are interdimensional.** There is a lot of healing work going on in the astral levels, where many are busy working in the night and wake up feeling bushed. There are also the schools in the etheric levels, where many go to learn, and this knowledge bleeds through into this dimension from the etheric levels of consciousness. This is often responsible for wisdom and abilities which seem to come from nowhere, and for drastic shifts in consciousness.

The most important thing to realize before you start interpreting your dreams is that they are *your* dreams. The meanings and symbols are for you, and though there are often symbols which are common, they may not mean the same to each individual.

The second tip in interpreting your dreams is to find out what type of dream it was and from where the message came. Was it from your own subconsciousness, was it prophetic, was it inspired by the Beautiful Many or from a lower level of consciousness? Was it literal or symbolic; and most important, is there a need for change or a healing?

These are all very important questions to ask when interpreting dreams. The next question most ask is, "How do I discern the type and meaning of a dream?" We can best answer this question with another question. From where did the dream come? It came from within. So what better place to start than within? MEDITATE. Go within and ask.

The best thing you can do for yourself is to establish conscious contact with your own inner guidance, the master teacher within. Not only do you have aspects of yourself existing on every level all the way back to creation, you also have the Beautiful Many waiting to assist you. Once you have established this connection, ask for a signal of their presence, along with yes and no signals. These signals can be used for discernment. They are very important in the days to come, because there will be a lot of experiences as the sensitivity of Humanity intensifies with the vibrational lifting.

As we have mentioned before, some experiences and connections are of a lower vibrational nature and need healing. That is where it becomes your responsibility to discern and feel the nature of an experience.

Establishing a strong connection within of the Highest Consciousness and Energy will be imperative in the awakening and healing process. Do not depend on others. They are only there to empower you to help yourself, and to support you in the process. Anything else is a dependency, and they are really helping themselves.

It is up to you whether you want to be a sovereign master, a dependent follower or remain in ignorance. Expand and empower yourself. You are worth it, for within you resides the gift of GOD—the one consciousness that encompasses all consciousness on all planes and all dimensions throughout the universe. Experience and master all of it. That is your destiny.

Mediocre Media

The media in general does not take you beyond the confines of social consciousness, and the better part is governed and controlled. This you need to know in the days ahead, because the very ground beneath your feet is going to shake. **There will be massive destruction due to the Earth**

---

changes around the world, and you will hear little or nothing about it, especially concerning how it all ties together. There will be mass sightings of UFOs and spiritual phenomena happening globally, yet it will go unannounced.

We talked earlier about the golden rule: "He who owns the most gold writes the rules." This also applies to the media. **Those who own the most gold also govern the media. You can control the people and alter destiny with knowledge which includes both information and disinformation,** and this is well known by those who own the most gold.

Those who own the most gold want to keep it, and that means business must continue as usual without interruption. It also means that the comfort zones remain in place, and they remain in control. **They can't control Nature or advanced civilizations which are both spiritually and technologically superior; therefore it is better to act as if everything is fine in the environment and the Earth change department, and say that those strange craft and lights in the sky, which are appearing on a grand scale, do not really exist.**

Think of the religious ramifications alone, when there is proof life began elsewhere billions of years prior to Earth. Adam and Eve will be upstaged, and the Earth will no longer be the center of the universe and the beginning of life. It never was!

It is also important not to release any information concerning free energy and alternative healing methods, again to maintain the status quo. How many grants do you think come from the government and big business? Where do colleges get most of their funding? Do you really believe they are going to promote something which is going to cut into their pocketbook? Hardly! Have you ever heard a politician get any air time who truly wants to abolish the status quo and serve the many over special interests? When was the last time you heard the main talking heads you trust to inform you tell it like it is, rather than how it is given to them?

Powerful heads of state, astronauts and high ranking

government officials in the know, as well as other professional people, are coming forward with knowledge concerning UFO cover-ups, sightings, encounters, black projects and a complete betrayal by our government of its people, yet they receive little or no coverage. Free energy devices are continuously being discovered and receive no press. The inventors can't get a patent or financing, and most end up disgruntled, paid off or dead. Meanwhile, we are up to our necks in radioactive waste, the air is foul, filled with carcinogens and petroleum by-products, and business goes on as usual.

If we continue business as usual, we are going to be out of business—socially, economically and as a species. The environment cannot sustain business as usual; therefore business as usual is going to be interrupted by forces that cannot be controlled by those with the most gold.

> *If we continue business as usual, we are going to be out of business—socially, economically and as a species.*

Are you going to be invaded? No. Are you going to be lifted up, and everything is just going to be hunky dory? No. Are the social, economic and physical Earth changes going to be accelerated? YES. Are you going to be divinely inspired and empowered within to get your lives and your environment in order? YES.

The information you need will come forward, as truth always does. Those who continue to act in their own self-interest at the expense of Humanity and Nature will be uncovered, and the reactions to their actions will also be accelerated. The talking heads, one by one, will be turned around by their own conscience, and those who don't will be left behind with egg on their faces and no credibility.

There are Grand Masters that can tell it to you like it is. They are not part of social consciousness. There are alternative newspapers, radio and television talk shows and functions where speakers are informing the public concerning what is going on behind closed doors and what those with the most gold don't want you to hear. Seek them out. Some are a little radical, swinging to the other side of the pendulum; yet if you take the middle path, you will have a good idea of what is truly happening in your world.

Don't take anything for granted. **The only source you can rely on is the source within. Use your own ability to discern and feel what is true for you.** When the talking heads tell you everything is fine (other than a few murders and a fire or two), and they switch to some political rally or the drama of some famous person, ask them about that hole in the ozone layer that is now bigger than all of Europe. Ask them about all those volcanoes going off, and the escalating earthquakes. Ask them about the erratic weather, the massive storms, flooding, hurricanes and tornadoes. Maybe it is time to ask them to cover these events and comment on the direction the Earth and its people are going? Maybe it is time we all just start thinking for ourselves?

There are two agendas concerning coming forward in the days to come. There is the agenda of those who would like to keep you in darkness and maintain the status quo. The second of is those who are bringing forward the truth, despite those who would like to keep you in darkness.

The deceivers have an impossible task in the days to come, and they know it; therefore they are leaking information a little at a time, letting the masses know, preparing them for that which is coming, not only in the form of Earth changes, but from the heavens. Very reluctantly and slowly, I might add, because it means giving up control and admitting to a grand deception which has lasted over 60 years.

There is a greater agenda with its own timetable which is rapidly unfolding concerning your brothers and sisters from the stars who have come to assist Humanity through these times of tumultuous change. Keep your eyes and ears open as well as your minds, and you will see it unfold. Everyone will!

3

Earth Renewal

Earth Change Update

In the days to come you are going to see amazing things. How each individual perceives and experiences these things is up to them. You are going to receive a crash course in how attached and material-minded you are, how much you love yourself and how deep your denial is.

To be enlightened is to be in knowledge of the whole truth, not half-truths. It is to see GOD in all things, the omnipresent Creator in all Creation, which includes you on every level of your being. You are going to be tested in each one of these venues. There is going to be movement, change and healing coming forward from within all Creation. There is a saying, "GOD works through mysterious ways," yet when one awakens one can see more of the mystery and the way in which it operates.

You live in an action/reaction world known as the plane of demonstration where consciousness creates reality. *As an eternal soul you chose this timeline on this plane of demonstration for a reason, and it is going to challenge you on every level.* In these challenges you have the choice to greet them as a God or a victim, or even somewhere in between.

There is no way we can give you an exact description of what is to come individually or collectively, because much of this depends on individual and collective choices. A good example is if suddenly you awoke to the fact that war

---

is in fact fulfilling one king or leader's desire for what another king or leader has, killing the other children of God in all their diversity. If you were to realize war has nothing to do with God, and the war profiteers are the only ones that win, and you choose not to participate, that choice completely changes your destiny. It also changes the destiny of those you would have inflicted pain, suffering and death upon, which you would be tied to karmically in future experiences. If a collective says, "No, we are not going to war," then that changes their destiny and the collective karma of a nation.

If everyone decided to forgive, release the past and move forward, honoring the universal principles necessary for a healthy society and environment, you would be on the path to Heaven on Earth. The same goes for the destruction and pollution of the environment. If one person decides to clean up their environment, gets the collective to work together and clean up their environment, and the collective demands their leadership to make this a priority, the Earth will not have to react to their actions and cleanse herself. The severity of the cleansing for Earth to continue to be the platform for life will be determined by the pollution and destruction.

There is a lot of help from higher levels to assist those who are choosing to be a part of the awakening and healing process. It is called divine intervention, and it is ready and waiting for those who want to release the past, forgive, and live a life of service to humanity and the Earth. This comes in the form of Angelic Guides, Ascended Masters and Spiritually and Technologically advanced off-worlders, some of which are your ancient ancestors. As the veils between worlds become thinner in the days to come you will be seeing a lot of them, especially what you term ETs and their craft. Many are here to assist, some are here to observe and are coming on line to assist, and some have been here that were not for your highest and best good. They are being removed.

There is a negative grid composed of consciousness and

energy which has stunted the evolution of Earth humanity, and within which the tyrants operate and manipulate through ceremony. These ceremonies are no longer effective, and the grid is being torn down and replaced with a higher frequency grid which no longer supports their base frequencies. **Those aligned with competition, greed and the lust for power and wealth at the expense of humanity and the Earth are becoming very confused and dysfunctional and their world, along with their actions, is being revealed.** The age of tyranny is coming to a close.

This timeline you have chosen (which you are now on, if you are reading this book) has a destiny of its own—an outline, so to speak. There have been many prophesies about these times. The mountains will tremble and shake, the skies will become like sackcloth, there will be wars and rumors of wars, all of which are manifesting to one degree or another and will come to pass.

There is a science to all of this for those who do not believe in prophecy. The prophecies were given in the past by those who knew the science. Every 120,000 years or so there is an event that is cyclic in nature, and it is fast approaching. There were other events in Earth's history—great wars with technologies far beyond those of today's, meteor strikes and other cataclysms such as massive volcanic blasts, tsunamis, pole shifts, ice ages, etc.—that hit what is best called the reset button for many civilizations.

The good news is that you are all back in your ascending spiral of evolution, and hopefully you will get it right this time. **The Earth will survive, cleanse herself and ascend to the next level,** yet whether or not

> *The Earth will survive, cleanse herself and ascend to the next level.*

you finish this ride is a personal and collective choice.

We spoke in the earlier prophesies of erratic weather,

drought in some areas, massive fires and floods in others. We spoke of a dramatic increase in tornadoes and hurricanes in number and severity. We spoke of the unprecedented increase in earthquake and volcanic activity, which has gone up 400% in numbers and severity. We spoke of the Sun and the mega cycles which are now upon you again with unprecedented solar flares and coronal mass ejections. What we have not spoken of to the masses is what is truly behind all of this, because most were not ready and it was too far off in the future.

Your solar system is entering a new place in the universe. You have been feeling the effects in your weather, earthquakes and volcanoes, as well as in the bioelectric fields surrounding the human and the Earth's body. **The entire galaxy is going through a grand shift.**

At the center of every universe is a black hole, spiraling out from which are the stars, planets and systems, such as the solar system in which you live. There are cycles in this rotation, and you are coming to the end of one such cycle that many refer to as the Great Shift or the Grand Cycle. **The gravitational energies you are moving into have the potential to create a pole shift.** The erratic weather, earthquakes and volcanoes above land and under the sea will continue to escalate as the solar system moves closer to this event. This pretty much makes war obsolete, and your energies could better be put towards preparation.

This is what the prophets were saying when they said that the mountains will shake and the land will tremble. **The Sun will become dark as sackcloth, caused by volcanic eruptions, impacts from meteors and cosmic dust.** Solar flares, coronal mass ejections and great gravitational waves from the Galactic Core have been the cause of these incoming meteors and cosmic dust.

The great wave vision given to many down under is not the tsunamis; it is a gravitational wave. **A pole shift would cause the oceans to reel across the continents, which would rise and fall in the process.** There are whole cities and temples built of stone to this day beneath your oceans that remain as a testimony to these events having occurred repeatedly in the past.

Before this event there will be many warnings. The erratic weather, droughts, fires, floods and the increase in severity and number of storms, tornadoes, typhoons, hurricanes, quakes and volcanoes, some of which are in the oceans, will continue to diminish the coastal populations. These are not bad people being punished by God; they are bad listeners caught unaware of the obvious and continuous warnings.

You have the ability to know your future. *You have the choice to prepare physically, mentally, emotionally and spiritually. You have divine intervention waiting to assist you in these endeavors. The choices you make will determine the outcome, yet denial is not a wise choice in these matters.*

The Beautiful Many are awaiting your choice. Now is the time to choose to live according to the universal principles and understandings necessary for a healthy society and environment. Learn to share, cooperate, prepare on every level and be a blessing to life.

Make your own personal God connection, and act on the inner guidance. It is all part of the ascension process. **Heaven is coming to Earth.** There will be a thousand years of peace, and humanity will once again live in harmony with each other and nature and join the rest of the universe in peace. **Do not be in denial of what is to come between now and then on this timeline** which this book, and you, are residing upon.

> *There are those conditions that in the activity of individuals, in the line of thought and endeavor, often keep many a land intact, through their application of spiritual laws in their association with individuals.*
>
> Edgar Cayce

Message from Gaia, "Mother Earth"

From the author: As I sat at my computer (yes I do use a computer, though the transmissions were hand written), the energy shifted and a new presence came upon me. It was overwhelming at first; yet as I became comfortable with the presence, I began to receive a wonderful love feeding, along with a transmission of information. I did not ask who it was; I just began to type as fast as I could.

After recording the transmission, I realized it was Gaia, the feminine spirit of the Earth, often referred to as Mother Earth. I felt her great love for Humanity and the Earth. I felt her sadness and her concern. I also felt her compassion and understanding, as well as why she must do what she needs to do. She asked that her message be a part of the book. Cazekiel also gave his overwhelming support. Later I found out he opened the door and stepped back, so to speak, to allow Gaia to give me the transmission. I hope it moves you as much as it moved me.

Beloved children, although you are all spirits who have come from many places, the body you inhabit is born of Earth. You are my children, just as all life is upon this plane, for I am the feminine spirit many of you refer to as Mother Earth.

I am ascending to a new level of consciousness, and the Earth will follow suit as a physical example of this consciousness. **It will be a rebirth, and all life will go through the birthing process.** Nature will reflect this process with its ever-changing weather patterns, earthquakes, volcanoes and rising tides. It will affect all species of life, the most drastic of which will be Humanity.

Humanity as a collective has lost touch with changing patterns and the evolutionary process of Earth. The rest of the animal kingdom is attuned to these changes and they are relocating, adapting and making adjustments to flow with these changes. **Unfortunately, the better portion of Humanity is oblivious to what is on the very near horizon.**

There are some who are aware of the changes in the land as well as in consciousness, yet their words go unheeded; and they are ridiculed and ignored by those who deem themselves to be civilized, especially those who are obsessed with continuing in a lifestyle that is destroying the very platform for life. They have found their comfort zone, yet in the future it will provide no security and be their greatest discomfort when all they have is torn asunder in the healing process. **This rebirth is necessary for Humanity to continue as a species and for me to also continue to provide the platform for life for Humanity.**

What your scientists are not telling you is that I am dying. I have been poisoned from the highest peaks to the deepest depths of my oceans. Where once great forests stood are barren wastelands, which is doing away with the very oxygen you breathe. The air and the water have become toxic and people are dying from birth defects, diseases and cancers directly related to these toxins. Your own immune systems are on overload and cannot keep up with the constant assault by these toxins. My immune system is also on overload, and I cannot heal myself fast enough to keep up with the constant assaults of Humanity, which are escalating to this day. This is why the changes are necessary.

I am not angry, nor am I punishing Humanity. I am doing my duty as a mother to protect and care for as many of my children as possible. I need your help. I need you to listen and to do as the animals are doing.

There will be places that you will have to move from because they will undergo severe changes in the healing process. I need you to go back to a more natural way of life. I need you to stop cutting down the forests and polluting the air and water. I also need you to stop warring on each other individually and collectively, for that too affects Nature's stability. **Most of all, I need your understanding, your prayers and blessings to do what I must do.**

I love you greatly, as a mother loves her children. My heart is heavy, because many of my children have forgotten their mother. They cannot hear my voice, and have chosen to ignore the warnings.

Many shall perish, yet their spirits are eternal and will learn from the experience. I will only reclaim that which I gave them, and that is life on this plane. **When they have learned their lessons, they will be allowed to return; and I will give them a new body, a body much more evolved.** They will be given a second chance on a new Earth, a planet where love has once again become the manifesting force behind all creation. Love of the inseparable oneness of GOD, Humanity and Nature, which are all part of the omnipresent universal life force, is love.

Your loving mother,
Gaia

A Path and a Way

There are solutions to social, economic and environmental problems dedicated to bringing peace, unity, equality and individual prosperity and freedom. One is a balanced way of living in harmony with Nature that promotes health and longevity. The balanced way ensures that individuals each reach their highest potential, giving back to the whole, allowing society to evolve to its greatest potential.

Defending names, images and doctrines has only resulted in separation, division and war. Rather than focus on the differences, in a more equitable approach to unity, peace and freedom, why not focus on the similarities? Only a limited God needs defending, and truth will always stand the test of time on its own merit. An apple is still an apple, no matter what you name it; you do not change its nature. **A call to spirit is always heard, no matter how it is made. God is multilingual, and there are many paths to God.**

The need to control and the endless power struggles

---

pitting Humanity against itself must discontinue. Neither religion nor any other teaching takes precedence over or supersedes the Law of Love. All else is in error. Every master, prophet, saint and sage had a deep, profound love for GOD, Humanity and Nature. They all agreed on certain Universal Principles and Understandings which are the unifying threads found in all religions, binding all cultures together.

It is the innermost desire for all Humanity to unify with their Creator and live a loving, joyous, prosperous life in peace and freedom. Let all the voices come together in praise of their Creator, each in his or her own unique way, as one great harmonic chord reverberating throughout the heavens. By allowing the differences, focusing primarily on the similarities and making the fulfillment of these innermost desires first priority, love, joy, unity, peace and individual prosperity and freedom will be the manifesting force behind all creation.

Religions must dispense with the images of wrathful Gods and tormenting devils, and in their place teach the action/reaction principle as well as the principles of accountability and responsibility. Fear, unworthiness, judgment, condemnation and guilt, which are the clouds that separate man from God, must be replaced with love, joy, compassion and forgiveness.

Man and woman are created equally, in the same image and likeness of God in spirit. They are divine, born out of the original light. Within every man and woman resides a loving, joyous, wise and powerful manifesting God waiting to unfold; an embryo waiting to be born. Meister Eckhart, a Christian theologian, said, **"If nut seeds produce nut trees, and pear seeds produce pear trees, then God seeds produce Gods."** What can a child of God grow up to be, other than a God or Goddess?

Beyond the body and personality lies all of creation. It is wise to follow the leads of the master teachers, and rather than worship their personalities, focus on the nature or ideal they represented, and find that nature or ideal within self.

Love God with all your heart, honor each individual as a unique expression of God, and behave as if the God in all life matters. *These three basic understandings, if taught and applied with impeccable integrity, will solve all the ills of Humanity.* Love must once again be the manifesting force behind all creation.

When addressing the mind, we must address the mental and emotional bodies. There are techniques dedicated to renewing the mind and bringing balance and stability into our daily lives. These techniques concern prayer, meditation, spiritual mind treatments, process-oriented therapies and various forms of counseling.

Ancient mystics in the East and West, as well as quantum field theorists, have come full circle in agreement that **consciousness creates reality.** We live in an ACTION/ REACTION world of self-created realities known as the

> *Ancient mystics and quantum field theorists agree: Consciousness creates reality.*

PLANE OF DEMONSTRATION where CONSCIOUSNESS CREATES REALITY. We manifest and magnetize people and events into our daily lives according to our consciousness. Our consciousness consists of our attitudes, emotions and beliefs in the world in which we live.

Most enlightened doctors on the forefront of medicine agree that **most diseases originate with an unresolved attitude, emotion or trauma.** There is a matrix of consciousness and energy beyond the physical, and **the physical body is only the hard copy of our mental and emotional bodies.**

All true and everlasting healing begins in consciousness, and in a holistic approach to healing, we must address the mental and emotional needs as well. There is documented scientific evidence which proves the physical effects of prayer and meditation, as well as the mind/body connection. Our inner world is just as important as our outer world. There is a saying, "Change your mind, change the world." *Through the use of prayer, meditation, spiritual mind treatments, process-oriented therapies and re-education, teaching and applying basic universal principles and life skills, we can alter the course of our destiny and create a better world individually and collectively.*

When addressing our physical body, we must address the Earth body as well. There is a symbiotic relationship and an intricate balance that must be maintained for a healthy environment.

We live in a series of interconnected systems. What is done to the least of life affects the whole. We must maintain and honor the diversity of life, and restore that diversity wherever it has been destroyed. There must be a balance between development and preservation. We can no longer afford the luxury of destroying our forests, as well as other habitats, and doing away with the diversity of life and the very oxygen we breathe. *The escalation in physical Earth changes is Nature's reaction to imbalances and warring against Nature, dishonoring the basic universal laws of Nature.*

Our mental, emotional and physical well-being depends upon a close connection with Nature. *Learn to grow your own food. Use organic fertilizers, remineralize the soil and allow the helpful predatory insects to do their work. Take liquid vitamin and mineral supplements in the meantime to bring back the mineral balance within your own body. There are also free radical scavengers and herbal formulas that will help remove the toxins from your bodies.*

Do not support those who are destroying our forests and other habitats by not using sound continuous yield procedures, dishonoring the diversity and balance of life. Do not support those who produce and use chemical fertilizers, herbicides and pesticides.

Take control over your own healing process. Do some research, especially in the field of alternative medicine. Look at the statistics and the results, and don't take anybody's word, despite their credentials; check out all your options. *Fresh air, pure water and vitamin and mineral-rich foods, exercise, nature walks, stress management, massage and classes in Tai Chi or Yoga, bringing awareness back into the body, will promote better health and longevity. Love your bodies, and the Earth body as well.*

There is a saying in Europe that a capitalist will sell the rope to hang himself. Capitalism without consciousness can be fatal. **As long as money is the decisive force and power governing the destiny of a civilization, without the highest and best good for Humanity and the Earth in mind, then eventually, there will be a collapse of that civilization.**

Those who have made their money at the expense of Humanity and Nature are setting themselves up for dire consequences concerning the future reaction by Humanity and Nature. It's time for them to contemplate how much gold it takes to exact self-worth. How many must they govern? When will they realize their next move depends upon the move of those they govern? Who is really governing whom, and who's controlling destiny? When will they realize that material acquisitions and outer appearances gained for respect, approval and acceptance outside of self will never be enough to make up for what they are lacking on the inside until they respect, approve and accept themselves? What good is gaining all the material acquisitions of the world and losing your soul?

Consider the karmic reaction for actions against Humanity and Nature, and the loss in evolution into the higher planes of love, joy, wisdom and power. In the eternal scheme of things, there is no gain, because you have to come back and do it all over again—only next time the lessons will be harder.

You came here to evolve, not devolve, and to be a blessing to life. *It feels much better and creates joy to direct one's time and energy towards the awakening and healing of Humanity and the Earth.* That is what you have been after all along: Love, Acceptance, Approval, Respect and Joy. Maybe up to now you have been going about it all wrong?

Material objects do not possess emotions; they come from within. Feelings about oneself are not something to earn or acquire, and are not dependent upon outer appearances or someone outside of self. They are something to accept within.

When you love, accept and approve of yourself, you are unshakable. You do not depend upon the acceptance and approval of others to establish self-worth, nor material acquisitions and outer appearances, which are transitory.

> *When you love, accept and approve of yourself, you are unshakable.*

Maybe it's time to simplify. It is time for those who have been blessed with abundance to reinvest in the awakening and healing of Humanity and the restoration of Earth. It is in arrogance and vanity that one separates himself or herself from the rest of Humanity and the environment.

It is in vain to believe one is separate from the action/reaction principle and the universal principle of accountability and responsibility. That is where the greatest insecurity arises.

There is no security in what you acquire; it is how you acquire it and what you do with it that brings security. What good is a castle surrounded by a cesspool, and where is the security and freedom when it is not safe to venture out from the castle?

The balance of power and wealth will be redistributed, willingly or unwillingly. It is the law of compensation. You cannot take from another anything which is not rightfully yours, or keep what is not. If we take something at the expense of another or Nature, without giving something of equal value, the same or equivalent will be removed from us in some way. Any short term gain will only result in a long term loss. This includes industries which perpetuate dependencies, continue to destroy our environment, and refuse to act in the highest and best good of Humanity and Nature.

We must take into account future generations in all that we do. **The children are the lineage and caretakers of the environment in which we will return.** How would you feel being raised by your children? What kind of environment are you leaving them? Do they know that consciousness creates reality? How about the action/reaction principle or the principle of accountability and responsibility? How about the other Universal Principles which are necessary for a healthy society and environment? Could they pass them on to you, or to their children?

How about investing in them? Why not educate them in the Universal Principles and life skills necessary for a healthy society and environment, rather than continuing to educate them in the other way, which has proven repeatedly to be dysfunctional?

There is one all-encompassing and all-inclusive Creator; name it what you wish. There is one race in all its diversity, and that is the human race. There is one planet we all share. The air, the water, the food that we eat, and life binds us all together. We are all in this together; and together, as long as we act upon the inspiration, we can make a difference. *"Everyone is chosen, yet few choose and have the integrity and courage to remain steadfast in that choice."*

Mystery Schools 2

In the preceding book [*Reunion with Source,* originally titled *Becoming Gods*], the mystery schools were covered, yet not to the extent which is necessary. **In today's standard curriculum, the majority of it is based upon recycled ignorance, theories and facts, most of which have been proven false.** The astronomy books will have to be rewritten after the Hubble telescope finishes revealing its information. The

---

geology books will also have to be altered after watching planets form from hot fiery gasses thrown from suns, the core of which continues to be hollow due to centripetal and centrifugal force spinning the heavier elements outward, creating the crust. The biology, chemistry and physics books will have to incorporate quantum field research proving the world we live in is actually nonmaterial. The religious books and history books will also have to be expanded because they only go back 4,000 years, with a lot of erroneous information.

Life on Earth has been destroyed many times by the use of atomic weapons by ancient advanced warring cultures and through natural disasters and cosmic events, such as the impact of comets and meteors. Your entire solar system has been rearranged on several occasions. The first colonies came from the stars over 28 million years ago. Atlantis and Lemuria and other past civilizations are not even mentioned in the standard curriculum, and how about all that forbidden archeology that keeps turning up? It blows apart the accepted theories which continue to be taught and enforced by the administrative hierarchy.

Life on Earth has been destroyed many times.

The pyramids were not constructed by a bunch of slaves in straw and mud pits. That's preposterous! People didn't roll the stones up into place with palm trees either; the trees could not withstand the weight. They are also much older than presumed. **The pyramids were ancient mystery schools, and only later were they used as tombs for the Pharaohs.** The immense blocks of stone were cut precisely with laser lights and placed with the use of anti-gravity.

Students today care very little about the history taught in school; they want to know about the pyramids, who built them, how and why. They want to know about Stonehenge and about Atlantis and Lemuria. They also want to know about Greek mythology, which wasn't really mythology. They want to know about ancient civilizations and what happened to them.

Even the religious books will have to finally admit that they were written in primitive times and maybe, just maybe, they didn't get all the facts right. Maybe the Earth is not flat, and so what if it isn't the center of the universe? So what if there are other galaxies out there, billions of years older than Earth, with suns and planets that can and do sustain life? So what if life did not begin on Earth? Everything else is right, and you shouldn't question God. How many complete contradictions and what else is it going to take?

How many kids are going to have to rebel or drop out because of boredom before we start listening to them? Where do you think they came from? **Kids know what's what in the universe, because it is written within their souls.** It is a feeling that tells them something is amiss. **There is a great need for the mystery schools to come once again, because of the blatant disregard for truth in today's standard curriculum, as well as the sheer boredom.**

The Universal Principles and Understandings necessary for a healthy society and environment also need to be taught. We have to be brutally honest with ourselves and look at the condition of our society and our environment and ask, "Is it working?" What has the past taught us, and what can we expect from the future if we continue on the same path? *What are our options, and is there another path, another way? There is, and the way is taught within the mystery schools.*

There is a way that will bring unity, peace, equality, prosperity and brotherly/sisterly love to all; a way that teaches the universal principles found throughout all cultures. There is a way that inspires individuals to reach the apex of their unique talents, abilities and purpose, giving back in service to the whole. *There is a way that allows both the individual and the collective to achieve their greatest potential; a way whose time is long since overdue. That is the purpose of the mystery schools.*

The other option is to continue business as usual in a way which is headed for social, economic and environmental collapse. These schools have been a part of history which is intentionally overlooked. The knowledge contained within these schools has continued to be passed down throughout history, and is found within ancient Sumerian, Egyptian, Hindu and Greek texts.

This knowledge was the founding principles of many of your greatest thinkers of the past. Pythagoras built the Pythagorean Society on these principles, which was an ancient mystery school. Plato and other great thinkers also derived their knowledge from these schools.

Throughout history these schools came and went, due to unscrupulous tyrants who were threatened by education and empowering of the masses. Knowledge is power, and they could not afford the masses to have access to more knowledge than themselves; therefore they did away with the schools and their teachers. Enlightened, empowered individuals in touch with their own Divinity cannot be controlled or held in subservience; therefore they did away with the schools.

These great Masters and teachers of the mystery schools are returning, seen and unseen, inspiring the masses above and below to recreate these schools of ancient wisdom. It is a force and power as never before seen upon the Earth, for this information is necessary for Earth to take its rightful place in the universe alongside its ancient ancestors in the stars. They have found peace, and it is also part of Earth's evolution to find that peace.

Light Centers of Higher Consciousness

As the Higher Consciousness and Energy increases upon this plane, there will be many physical anchors upon the Earth to maintain and usher in this new Consciousness and Energy. Many of these centers will be located upon

---

leylines or grid points, which will enhance their ability to affect the planet.

Some of these leyline intersections or grid points are already inhabited by orthodox religions, which are there, not in the highest and best good for Humanity and the Earth, but have been placed there for control. When the Higher Consciousness and Energy comes in, they believe (in error) that they will have control over it.

Power and control are what drive them. What they don't realize is that they are out of alignment or do not have the proper consciousness to direct or control these energies, and they will instead experience amplified chaos in their lives.

All of their imbalances will come forward, as well as their lust for power and the greed within their very own ranks, and their true motives and intentions will be seen for what they are. There will be those within their own ranks who are going to not only turn around, but turn on them, because of their own conscience and the desire to make restitution. This is already happening.

These orthodox religions will employ their black operatives, as they have in the past, to do away with these brave souls, yet it will be to no avail, because there will be too many of them. The same drive to serve and experience God will drive these courageous souls to expose and put an end to those who create the ultimate blasphemy, which is to use GOD's name to intimidate and perpetuate fear, unworthiness and guilt, and to extort money from those who have very little.

This will all be accelerated, amplified, and everything where love is not the manifesting force behind attitudes, emotions and actions will be exposed. The action/reaction principle will also be accelerated, and those who continue to cause pain, suffering or loss to others will have the same meted out to them in equal measure almost instantaneously. As you can see, for them it is not an option; they must also come into alignment with the new Higher Consciousness and Energy or suffer greatly at their own hands.

The new centers coming forward will also have to keep a constant vigil on their motives and not stray from the first cause, which is to serve Humanity and Nature, ushering in the new Higher Consciousness and Energy. They need your support; if it wasn't for them, the collective consciousness would have collapsed on this plane years ago.

They come in all colors, shapes and sizes, they are diverse in culture and language, and all have one thing in common: a great love for GOD, Humanity and the Earth. They operate under the Laws of Creation, which often conflict with the powers that be, the laws of man and the status quo. They stand for brotherly/sisterly love, joy, peace, equality, individual freedom and prosperity for all. They do not believe in separation, judgment or condemnation. They allow. That is why they are such a threat.

The powers that be do not believe in equality; their very existence depends upon maintaining a hierarchy and not only keeping you divided, but against each other. Divide and conquer is part of their modus operandi, and peace also is a threat, because unity often follows peace.

They do not believe in brotherly/sisterly love, because love to them is sense gratification and ownership. Their love depends upon the object of their love serving them and behaving according to their rules, regulations and expectations. It is very, very conditional love. Their love does not extend beyond their own families and a few—very few—friends who match their own consciousness. Everyone else is fair game.

Their existence also depends on the continuation of actions which exploit both Human and Natural resources. The enlightened ones are a sore reminder that there will be consequences. As you can see, enlightened masters and the new centers of Higher Consciousness and Energy have a lot stacked against them, and need your support.

There are many who will say, "Why should I support these centers? What is in it for me?" **Right now your very survival is going to depend upon a lot of divine intervention and the work of these centers.**

Consciousness creates reality, and for every action there is a reaction. Through divine intervention and grace, the consciousness and the reactions to actions against Humanity and Nature can be cleaned up. **Through prayer, meditation and the healing of negative influences, these centers provide an invaluable service to Humanity and the Earth.** There are those who say, "If I cannot eat it, hold it in my hand or use it to further my material existence, it is of no value."

Your very material existence depends upon their work. What good are all of your material acquisitions if the very platform for life ceases? What if the consciousness collapses into complete decadence, competition, war and base survival? What if Nature's reaction was unleashed in its entirety, without the saving grace which has so generously been bestowed upon you? Many have no idea concerning the divine intervention which has already occurred on their behalf to save a race bent upon not only destroying themselves, but the very platform for life.

> *What good are all of your material acquisitions if the very platform for life ceases?*

If you were to shift dimensions to a level where you could rise above the Earth and see clairvoyantly the centers and Grand Masters walking the Earth, you would see brilliant multicolored lights emanating from them. They are feeding and holding together the consciousness upon this plane. Their numbers are increasing exponentially, and you just might be one of them. Very few are aware of what is being done on the outskirts of their auras.

Those who are aware and are consciously engaging the light and sending it out, are increasing the effect a thousand-fold. The Grand Masters and Avatars are increasing the effect a million-fold. This is growing exponentially as more awaken and become enlightened.

Ascension into the next level of consciousness is unavoidable, and it is a race between awakening and healing the past gracefully, or experiencing the reaction in its entirety. Those who choose to continue in the old ways and work against or resist the Higher Consciousness and Energy, as well as their own evolution, will experience pain, suffering and loss, or succumb to the diseases and reactions to their actions.

This is not the wrath of GOD. GOD loves them unconditionally. It is Nature's way to ensure evolution, and the consequences of going against the Laws of Creation. It is done by their choice and at their hand. They are punishing themselves. They can make different choices aligned with the Laws of Creation and act in the highest and best good of Humanity and Earth. They can make restitution, redirect their time, energy and resources, and through grace and forgiveness heal the past. In a moment, they can change their destiny. It is up to them, as it always has been.

When you live in an action/reaction world known as the plane of demonstration where consciousness creates reality, you have to be careful. You can hurt yourself. Through the pain, hopefully, comes the birth of wisdom. Now that you know what you don't want, release it and start creating what you do want.

The Laws of Creation are there to ensure evolution and keep you from directing your energies in a way that would create devolution or bring continuous harm to Humanity or Nature. They also take into account the fact that you are eternal, and if it takes death to bring you a lesson, so be it.

You can come back and do it all over again, build your castle at the expense of Humanity and Nature, experience the pain, suffering and loss you have meted out to others in equal measure, and eventually lose everything. You can do it repeatedly, as many of you have. The only change is, this time you will have to do it somewhere else. **You won't be able to return to Earth, because the vibration will have lifted out of your reach and the very cell itself will not allow you to return.**

Now is the time to take stock of your attitudes, emotions and actions. It is a time to heal and surrender to your own God selves, which will allow you the wisdom and the grace necessary to heal. It is time to make restitution for actions against Humanity and Nature, and support the light workers and the centers which are working arduously to clean up the consciousness and the reactions upon this plane. The work they are doing is invaluable, and they need your support on every level. The powers that be and the status quo are going to resist the light workers and the centers, because they are a sore reminder of what is being done at the expense of Humanity and Nature.

Those at the centers do not live according to the accepted standards of society. *They live according to the Laws of Creation, which supersede and often conflict with the laws of man. It is often the unjust laws of man that see to their demise.*

There is one law that no law supersedes, and that is the Law of Love. They stand for brotherly/sisterly love, joy, peace, equality, individual freedom and prosperity for all— things the powers that be and the status quo have forgotten, are in denial of, and often resist vehemently. Their greatest denial is the reaction which is fast approaching on the horizon. The heavenly hosts, Angelic Guides, Ascended Masters and the consciousness and energy of the very Source itself are behind this event.

You are going to see the end of denial, and a lot of humility, in the days to come. The days of the tyrants are coming to a close. Each and every one of you has a personal invitation to be exalted into the Highest Consciousness and Energy, which is unconditional love and joy; "Bliss." Become a light worker and support the centers which are anchoring in the Higher Consciousness and Energy.

Then there is option number two: the powers that be, social consciousness, and those who will continue to act arrogantly and selfishly against Humanity and Nature. There are also those who have turned a blind eye and continue to support the powers that be, intellectually validating what they know in their souls to be wrong. Some even do it for security. There is no security in aligning with this group, because you will suffer the reaction to their action by your involvement and your attachment.

The choice by now should be very obvious. Choose Love, and always act in the highest and best good of Humanity and the Earth. It is also wise to stand behind and support those who have also made this choice, as well as the centers which are cleaning up the consciousness and energy upon this plane. **Support those who are empowering and educating the individual for a better tomorrow.**

A Master's Journey

In a far-away galaxy, a great light heard a plea for help from a civilization that was destined for social, economic and environmental collapse. They had strayed so far from the basic Universal Principles and Natural Laws of Creation that they did not know how to return. They had forgotten.

They had given their power away to religions and governments, hoping they would show them the way and take care of them, only to have their trust betrayed and their power used against them. Each religion and government had its way—it was the only way—and they divided themselves in endless power struggles and conflicts, defending their names, images, doctrines and borders.

In their quest for unconditional love, joy, peace and individual freedom and prosperity, they found separation, division and war, as well as a love that was very conditional and a loss of individual freedom and prosperity. They searched the mountaintops, went to leaders and teachers, traversed rivers and crossed oceans, all in the search for God and the way. For hundreds of years they searched in vain, and all the while the great light watched.

The great light sent inspiration, love, joy, wisdom and

power, yet few could receive. His great love and compassion, along with his desire to help, became so overwhelming, he decided to incarnate into the civilization. This way he could teach them and live his teachings as an example. He could speak to them in a physical voice to ensure that they heard. He would be an example so they could see with their physical eyes, and he could be close to them so they could feel his love, joy and compassion.

He felt that surely once the message was delivered in the physical they would remember their Divinity and apply the Universal Principles and Natural Laws of Creation in their everyday lives. This would put an end to the separation, division and war, as well as the destruction of the very platform for life. He thought surely they would discontinue warring upon each other and their environment, and choose a path that would bring love, joy, peace, prosperity and individual freedom to everyone, especially considering the social, economic and environmental collapse which was just around the corner.

He was born innocent, with the Universal Principles and Natural Laws of Creation burning within his heart. He was fully aware of other planes and dimensions, extremely sensitive and aware of the intentions of others, especially those whose words did not correspond with what they were thinking and what was within their hearts.

He was raised in a small desert community. He spent hours sitting upon giant granite boulders looking out across the desert, often sleeping outside under the desert skies. He contemplated the nature of GOD, the heavens, life and the way people treated each other.

He did not understand why people were not honest with each other, why they tried to control and manipulate each other, and where that drive for money above all else came from. He saw people searching for security, acting selfishly against Humanity and Nature, forgetting the basic action/reaction principle, which became their greatest insecurity.

He watched as they brought pain and suffering upon

themselves again and again without learning the lesson. He knew they were not evil; they just didn't understand the Universal Principles and Natural Laws of Creation.

Finally he decided it was time to go forward and teach what he came to teach, and live his teachings as an example. He knew it would not be easy. He remembered the fate of the other prophets, saints and sages throughout the many cultures, some of which he himself taught and inspired. He watched those who persecuted and killed them, falsified their teachings, and incorporated them as idols into their own institutions. He watched many of them die with bent backs and broken hearts, carrying the karma of others they loved, only to be betrayed by them in the end.

Those he taught and inspired each had a deep and profound love for GOD, Humanity and Nature, and held steadfast to the Law of Love which supersedes the laws of kings, religions and governments. He watched as kings, religions and governments continued to exalt themselves above that law. He watched as their unbridled greed and lust for power at the expense of Humanity and Nature became insatiable. He hoped that his love, compassion and wisdom would overcome the fear, unworthiness, ignorance, religious and superstitious dogmas and self-destructive actions against Humanity and Nature.

What he didn't count on was the extent of the resistance, dishonesty, deception and betrayal he would encounter. He also was not prepared that most would choose outer appearances and the material as first priority over their inner quality and spiritual nature, intellectually justifying attitudes, emotions and actions they knew in their hearts to be wrong.

His love, joy, compassion and his life became a divine mirror. His presence amplified and accelerated the fear, unworthiness and opposition, as love often does. There were many who were secretly envious and jealous of him, and those who, rather than own their own reflections and iniquities, chose to project their demons and unresolved issues upon him.

There were those who feared losing their power, positions or wealth gained at the expense of Humanity and Nature, and those whose lives depended upon continuation of the status quo. There were even those who feared the wrath of God for even talking to him. They feared change, the unknown, and were very insecure.

All in their own way decided to judge, condemn and demonize him, spreading vile rumors and gossip, never contemplating the fact that their efforts not only went against Christianity but also against being a decent human being.

He told the rich they were not separate from Humanity and Nature; they needed to reinvest back into their communities, their environment, and it was no longer appropriate to act in any way at the expense of Humanity and Nature.

He told the poor they needed to start loving themselves, release their unworthiness and poverty consciousness, and start manifesting and believing in themselves. He told the victims they were not victims, to heal their fears and to stop using their self-created realities to gain either financial or emotional support from others, and to start manifesting.

He told the saviors to stop saving the victims and allow them to evolve and gain the wisdom from their self-created realities. He told the persecutors to heal their wounds, traumas and angers, and stop blaming or taking it out on others. He cautioned each on the victim/savior/persecutor triangle, and not to get in it or perpetuate it.

He told the women to forgive the men, and stop denying their own masculine, objective side. *He told the men to honor women,* as well as their own feminine, subjective nature, and to stop abusing women and treating them as objects and possessions, rather than as equals.

He told the red man to forgive the white man, and to remain steadfast in the quest for Spirit and love for Nature. *He told the black man to forgive the white man* for enslaving them in the past, and to continue striving for freedom and equality. *He gave thanks to the migrant workers for harvesting the fields,* and inspired them also in their quest for dignity and equality. *He told the white man to end all discrimination, injustices and inequalities,* and to start helping those less fortunate.

He told the environmentalists that their attitudes and emotions were just as toxic and destructive as the actions of those they warred upon. He inspired them to speak their truth, yet remain steadfast in love. He told those who were destroying the environment to walk softly, and honor the diversity of life. He would not war nor side with anyone, neither condemning nor condoning their actions; thus he was hated by all but a few who knew the wisdom in his teachings.

He told everyone to be kind, not only to others, but to the environment as well. To bring love into each moment, and if they fell in consciousness, to try again until they remained steadfast in love. In each case, he planted a seed, in full awareness that one day that seed would grow. He knew that nothing could stop that seed from growing, and like the mighty oak, it would come forward, pushing everything out of its way.

He finally retreated to the mountains. For years he watched those he had touched war and bicker. He watched them continue to defend their names, images, doctrines and beliefs. He watched them judge, condemn and discriminate against each other. He watched them act selfishly, not only warring upon each other, but the very platform for life.

He watched the manifestations of their attitudes and emotions come forward, and reactions to their actions come full circle. He knew this all was necessary. It was the fertilizer that allowed the seeds to grow. Those who resisted the growth only continued creating more pain and suffering, more fertilizer.

Those who accepted the seeds and grew with them were exalted to new heights of Love, Joy, Wisdom and Power. They became like the mighty oak, and began spreading their own seeds. *He continued to inspire them from afar,* hoping that one day he could walk among the mighty oaks in full bloom.

Becoming Gods

4

Outrageous Understandings Beyond Belief

"Wisdom you need to know, yet probably aren't ready for."

A Hollow Earth

Within the ancient legends of your Indian and Nordic lore are stories concerning a paradise existing not on the surface of your planet, but within. There are ancient stories of a great flood and the breaking up of the lands, and an adventure inward to escape the catastrophes. There are myths about small green people that can appear and disappear, large giants eight to ten feet tall, and light beings that are more energy than physical. This next truth is so outrageous we will probably lose a few of you, yet that is always a gamble when stretching human consciousness.

YOUR EARTH IS HOLLOW. Now if that has not shocked you enough, it is also INHABITED.

In the first book [*Reunion with Source*, originally titled *Becoming Gods*], on the first page, we spoke of the birth of planets. They are born of the suns in a tremendous explosion of energy, after which hot swirling gasses find a cradle orbit around the sun. The gasses begin to cool, and the heavier elements are thrown to the outside, forming a crust due to the nature of centrifugal force and the pushing influences of the other planets. This process forms a hollow sphere with a central sun.

Your scientists have watched the birth of planets and are

very aware of this process. They have photographed nebulae, which consist of a shell forming around a central star. This is the second stage of the birth of a planet. As they observed other planets further along in their development, they observed cracks in the not yet solidified crust, with light shooting out the cracks. It was also shooting out the poles.

Through these observations, they came to the conclusion that planets are formed first from a hot gaseous star thrown from a sun into a cradle orbit; the shell is created due to natural forces of gravity, centripetal and centrifugal force, and the poles remain open. It is more like a flattened sphere bulging at the equator, with openings that lead to a hollow interior at the poles.

Mercury, Mars and Venus have all been observed to have light emitting from the poles. This is due to the central sun or the remnants of the star at the center of the planet, which formed them. When Mercury passes in front of the Sun, what should be a completely black disk has a great light shooting out the center as bright as the Sun. Once you pass 83 degrees of latitude on the Earth, compasses don't work. Why? Because the true North Pole is not a landmark. Once you pass 80 degrees, you begin a long decent into the interior, and the poles are above you.

The Earth's polar openings are over 1,400 miles wide, and as you descend, it is so gradual many are not aware they are going from one world to another. The only difference is that the sun never sets; it has a smoky hue, and there is no night and no stars.

There are many recorded expeditions where it is well-documented that as one goes further north or south to the Poles, after 70 to 80 degrees it starts getting warmer. The snow is covered with pollen in various colors, and the pollen increases as you venture further towards the Poles. The waters begin to melt, and warm winds begin to blow.

After a long, arduous journey, what should be getting increasingly frigid and void of life becomes quite the contrary. Vegetation and animal life increase as you venture further towards the Poles. When this happens, explorers believe they are lost, going in the wrong direction. They cannot depend upon their compasses, and eventually return. They were not equipped to handle the unexpected water. Many are too embarrassed to tell what happened, and others fabricate a story about a death-defying journey, braving frigid conditions a lesser man could never endure, eventually reaching the pole upon which they planted their flag.

The only way they could truly plant their flag on the Pole would be to attach a balloon to it, because the Pole is a point in the sky, not on the Earth. As one descends into the polar openings, the compasses begin to spin, because the poles are not in front of them but above them.

Many animals have been observed to migrate further north in the winter. Icebergs which consist of fresh water created from the rivers flowing from the poles are filled with tropical vegetation and debris.

Scientists to this day have no idea how these enormous fresh water icebergs form, because the rainfall and snow is minimal and nowhere near enough to continue to form these gigantic icebergs. This is all very unnerving, because it means the geology and astronomy books will have to be rewritten, and those in charge of your education will have egg on their faces. It also means a lot of formidable professors will have to give up their theories, which are taught as facts, and upon which they base their reputations.

There was a time when the Earth was believed to be flat because the Bible referred to the four corners of the Earth, and anyone who sailed too far out into the oceans would fall off the edge into space. Columbus found some ancient maps used by the Greeks which showed the Earth to be round and showed other unknown continents.

Of course, these continents were not unknown to the people who lived there, as well as to other explorers who were not Catholic. It is quite arrogant to claim to discover and lay claim to a continent which is already inhabited and visited frequently by other sailors. It was not blasphemous for the other sailors to talk about other continents they had explored which did not fit within the opinions of the church. Columbus listened to these explorers, read books which were not accepted curriculum, and due to the fondness of the queen and the promise to return with exotic spices and gold, was granted the ships to prove his theories. The church felt as though it was blasphemous, but figured he would fall off the edge anyway, and they would be done with it.

Another pioneer was Galileo, who used much of the data gathered by Copernicus, and postulated that the Sun was the center of the universe. At the time, the Earth was established as the center of the universe—after all, creation began on Earth, and everything had to revolve around Earth. This arrogant position discredits other galaxies created billions of years before Earth, and it would be very unnerving to find out there were other civilizations billions of years older than Humanity. The church labeled Galileo as a heretic, and because of his blasphemy he was excommunicated. They wanted to have him beheaded or thrown in jail, yet he had friends in high places, and eventually he was confined to house arrest.

The discovery of the Inner Earth will meet the same resistance, from the same establishments, and it will have the same impact the discoveries of the Earth being round and not the center of the universe had. *The next time someone tells you the Earth is solid or filled with molten rock, ask them if they have been there.*

This hollow sphere upon which you reside has an interior similar to your exterior. The interior has mountains, great lakes, rivers and a smoky sun, which is the remnant of the hot fiery gases which were the beginnings of the Earth.

The sun within the interior is approximately 600 miles in diameter. There is approximately 3,000 miles between the sun and the Inner Earth. It would be as if you were on the exterior on a cloudy day without a nightfall, and the only thing missing would be the stars.

There is pressure pushing outward from the central sun,

along with centrifugal force, which creates the gravity. The molten rock within the Earth's crust, which is approximately 800 miles thick, is created from the pressure pushing downward from the exterior and outward from the interior.

You are basically hollow, because of your digestive tract and lungs, and you have blood vessels running throughout your body, along with holes to take in and eliminate air, food and water. The Earth operates in much the same manner.

To some, this will give the Gaia principle (which postulates the Earth to be a living, conscious entity) a whole new meaning. Your government is very aware of the Inner Earth, and it is also a very big embarrassment to them. They have had very secret meetings concerning THE ENEMY WITHIN. **Everything your government cannot conquer, control or understand becomes the enemy;** and if they are powerless to do anything about this, they must keep it a secret. After all, aren't they the ones who are paid to protect you?

Nonetheless, those within are not your enemy; they are your brothers. They are a collective of an ancient race of beings from a distant galaxy and those who ventured inward during the great

> *Those within the Hollow Earth are not your enemy; they are your brothers.*

floods which sank Atlantis and Lemuria. They are a very diverse culture, and range in height from 3 to 12 feet tall.

There are also a few of your survivors who disappeared in the Bermuda triangle due to being caught within a great door opening within the ocean. **The technology of those within the Earth far surpasses the surface dwellers,** which is how they refer to you.

They can alter time, distance and space. They can make you see and feel holographic images that aren't really there. They can send your submarines and explorers on wild goose chases and lead them to believe they went to the North Pole.

Anyone who depends upon compasses and instruments to tell them where they are can be easily misled.

They are quite ingenious. They have great ships that defy gravity, with other smaller ships that can go from one end of the universe to the other in a blink of an eye. They can teleport objects, including themselves, in an instant. They can even shift dimensions. This is very embarrassing to your government.

They allowed several men to make the journey inward. The most recorded man in history was Admiral Byrd. His diaries will come forward in the near future. There have been several others, but this one is the most documented. Rather than release the information to the public, he was branded as a lunatic and kept drugged and locked up in an asylum—all in the interest of national security. They continued to have their secret meetings concerning claiming the new lands, not knowing that their meetings were never secret. Their plans were always known by those in the unseen, and found quite humorous.

These beings within the Earth are very loving, gentle beings. They have experienced thousands of years of peace; thus they have evolved both spiritually and technologically far beyond those on the surface. **They want to reunite with the rest of Humanity,** yet Humanity on the surface has to grow up. You must have a consciousness of peace and harmlessness before the door will open.

They will be very active in the future. Their presence will be seen in your skies and in your oceans. The Poles will open upon the melting of the caps.

There will be phenomena beyond your wildest dreams occurring in your very near future. They will be a large part of this phenomena, joined by other brothers from distant galaxies. These brilliant beings are very concerned with Humanity, for what Humanity does to the Earth affects them. There are oceans within the Inner Earth, great lakes and rivers connected to the surface.

There are doorways between these two worlds that open occasionally, and ships emerge to survey the damage being done on the surface. There are openings in both the North and South Poles; there is one in Mount Shasta, The Superstitious Mountains, Tibet and The Bermuda Triangle, as well as other smaller openings. The disappearances of planes and ships in the Bermuda Triangle are a direct result of the opening of a great doorway. These planes and ships are laid out in nice neat rows on a sandy beach within the interior. Those who survived the shock are still living harmoniously within. They can leave, but choose to stay.

Those within the interior share your water and your air, and your surface is their heaven. Needless to say, what Humanity on the surface has done to the air and water has them very concerned. What concerns them most are the nuclear tests, which are fracturing the Earth's crust in their heavens. The stored energy of these blasts is being released along the fault lines, which is making what would have been gradual adjustments known as earthquakes much more severe. There is a limit to allowing, and your governments have tested that limit to the maximum.

Further tests will have severe consequences, and an ultimatum has been delivered after many warnings went unheeded. Humanity's constant assaults on the Earth, poisoning the oceans and the air, and the nuclear testings, are affecting them.

Ambassadors from the interior have met with many people, including some within your government, in an attempt to bring awareness to the situation, and there has been some cooperation. Unfortunately, the major industries have too much power to block the necessary changes. Most of these major industries responsible for the pollution are located along the coasts and rivers. When the Earth changes begin, they will be the first to go. Those within the interior are well aware of the future, and pray Humanity learns from much of which they set into motion.

After the changes, there will be new governments. They will be established upon peace, unity and cooperation. This will open the door to the interior, and the exterior known as space. **Those within the interior are united with a federation of civilized planets that have watched over Humanity for eons,** allowing the Earth to evolve and learn from the reactions to their actions. The sooner the world chooses peace, the sooner this will occur.

Do not be surprised if in your dreams and meditations an ambassador short in stature, yet powerful in consciousness, appears to you by the name of Debeg. He will come with flashing eyes and a loving but very concerned and down-to-business look on his face. He brings with him a warning that now is the time to wake up and get on with cleaning up your act. They are very aware of the reactions on the horizon to the actions of their brothers on the surface. They have a great love for Humanity and are endeavoring to save Humanity from doing itself in. They have learned from their mistakes and have preserved their environment.

There are great forests and lakes within the interior which have been preserved. Many of your mythological creatures of the past exist there to this day.

There will come a time when this will be open, so to speak, to those who have the right consciousness. When the collective consciousness is sufficiently lifted, it will be open to everyone. This will come after the Earth changes, the fall of governments bent upon secrecy, war and againstness, and the completion of the vibrational lifting.

They want to live in peace and harmony with the rest of Humanity. They want to share their technology, their art and their way of life. They have no religions, no wars and no class separation, nor do they lack for anything. They honor the God within each other and the whole of life. That is why they are so advanced spiritually and technologically.

Rather than spending so much time and energy defending borders and struggling for power, they diverted their energies for the good of the whole. They have had thousands of years of peace devoted to the highest and best good of their race and their environment. It would be wise for those on the surface to contemplate that same direction.

The Constants

In the beginning, when the Source of all that is, the one consciousness that encompasses all consciousness, decided to expand, there was a tremendous explosion of light, and born were the Creator Gods. You were all originally conceived this way, yet because of many journeys into the flesh and many previous incarnations, you have forgotten your divine origin.

Not all the Creator Gods chose to incarnate. Many remained as light beings, observing the comings and goings from another frequency or dimension. They remain changeless, and still possess all of the love, joy, wisdom and power bestowed upon them by the first cause, the Source referred to as the supreme intelligence, GOD.

They experienced everything you experienced vicariously through you, but never incarnated; thus they maintained their position in the higher realms of consciousness. **There was a time when those who chose to incarnate stayed in contact with the heavens, and there was constant telepathic communication.**

Just as GOD experiences self through the many expressions of self, which includes all life on all planes and all dimensions, the Creator Gods had the same capabilities. **Over the years and after many incarnations, those who chose to incarnate began to experience separation from the higher planes of consciousness.** They experienced fear, guilt, unworthiness and doubt, and continued to add these lower vibrational attitudes and emotions to their consciousness, making it harder and harder to access the higher planes and dimensions.

Because of their inability to return to the highest realms of consciousness, lower realms needed to be created. After all, we just couldn't leave them dangling in space. As the consciousness of those who chose to incarnate collapsed further in consciousness due to the lower vibrational attitudes and emotions they accepted to be their reality, more planes and dimensions had to be created. These are often referred to as the wheel of life or the astral levels, yet there are other levels of consciousness beyond them.

So now you have GOD (the first cause), the Creator Gods, other planes and dimensions, and those who reside within them. IT'S A BIG UNIVERSE!

The Constants (the Creator Gods) who have remained in the highest planes are the great overseers. They are joined by the Beautiful Many Christed Masters, who ascended back into the Highest Consciousness by awakening to their true heritage. They transcended the lower vibrational attitudes and emotions.

The Christ Consciousness is the level where man knows self to be GOD, and GOD knows self to be man. It is the union or oneness with GOD, the absence of fear and unworthiness, where the false belief of separation ends.

When we refer to man, it includes all mankind. There are also Christed women and entire civilizations expressing the Christ Consciousness. There are spiritually and technologically advanced civilizations existing on other planes and dimensions; some are extraterrestrial, and some exist on this plane and dimension. These are all in alignment with the first cause, and are doing their part in the vibrational lifting and healing process.

There are those within the astral levels also, along with some very self-serving extraterrestrials, who are not part of the awakening and healing process; in fact, some are very against it. They have a lot of their own healing to do.

They vary in degrees of consciousness. Some are malevolent, very controlling and manipulating, and are possessive influences. Some also try to influence others, but not as aggressively.

There are faker spirits who will tell you they are this master and that master, and there are extraterrestrials who will claim to be your Creator, and that you owe your existence to them. There are even extraterrestrials who have claimed an alliance with saints and sages, and project their images to various people to get them to be subservient, yet this is very uncommon, because most of these have been turned around or removed. **You owe your existence to the GOD within, the life force. It is the same life force to which they owe their existence.**

There are also teachers and healers on the higher astral levels, yet they are limited by their own belief system. They are not yet Christed.

As your sensitivity increases, you are going to be more aware of these other planes and dimensions and those who reside upon them, the higher and lower vibrational ones. You are going to have to learn to use your own inner sensitivity, along with a few basic understandings, to keep yourself centered in your own Divinity. Use unconditional love, joy, unity and individual freedom as tools for discernment.

Do not give your power away to a subservient position. **Serving GOD is honoring the God within all life, despite color, belief and form.** It is honoring the God within you also, and the inseparable oneness of all life. GOD is love, and when you are one with love, you are one with GOD. It is that simple.

You don't need to read endless doctrines or worship endless names and images to find the God within you. **You are becoming what you have been all along, and only have to awaken and remember.** You are Gods and Goddesses, born of the original light, from which nothing was withheld. You are much more than a body and a personality that can be easily controlled and intimidated; **you are the Creator Gods who got lost in their own creation.**

This is the message that GOD (the first cause), the Creator Gods and The Beautiful Many Angelic Guides and Ascended Masters are delivering to you. They are bringing this consciousness back by popular demand. They are with legions, and those legions consist of other spiritually and technologically advanced beings, most of whom are your extraterrestrial ancestors.

UFOs Past, Present and Future

There have been ancient ships that precede any of your recorded history, which is a very short period when one looks at the big picture. There have been entire civilizations on Earth that were much more advanced than your present civilization. These civilizations have come and gone, due to wars and natural cataclysms.

The Earth is a melting pot or combination of several races which colonized the Earth millions of years ago. This is from where the diversity comes. Each race has descendants from the stars and has been forced to begin again as primitives, due to the wars and natural cataclysms.

The first visitors were from Lyra, a civilization of technologically advanced warriors who continuously destroyed their colonies due to power struggles within their own ranks. It was very small, the Earth was very primitive, and it didn't last long.

The Lyrians would often begin their colonies with good intentions, but their efforts almost always ended up in cataclysmic wars or natural disasters brought on by their own warring consciousness. Such was the fate of the first colony, which was lost in what would be termed "the wars in the heavens."

The Lyrians tried several other times to colonize Earth. Their civilizations rose to great heights, only to destroy themselves with weapons so powerful they left the Earth almost completely uninhabitable. Their best attempt was the civilizations known as Atlantians from Atlantis and Lemurians from Lemuria, or Mu.

These were colonies which again originated from Lyra, yet this time it was the peaceful Lyrians fleeing the wars who had settled into the Pleiades, Orion and Haydes systems. We are using these constellations as known reference points closest to where they reside, such as the Pleiades, which in truth is a series of young blue suns and is not inhabitable.

The Pleiadian/Plejaran people actually live on a planet called Erra in the Tayget system, which exists in another dimension of time. Because there are no reference points, we will continue to use the commonly accepted and known constellations and names such as Pleiadian, Orion and Andromedan.

The Lyrians went through evolutionary changes on planets within these systems before returning to once again colonize the Earth. They were very advanced and had mastered laser light technology with crystals, anti-gravity and time travel, and had great ships capable of mass destruction as well. They lived in peace for thousands of years, which attracted other civilizations from the stars to also settle on the Earth.

The Black race was a peaceful and very spiritual group which came from Sirius. The Yellow race also came during this time. They were a very ancient race and set up their own colonies in seclusion in Asia. They are very protective about their ancient roots, and little is known about their origin. This was wise, because when one is exploring other galaxies there is the chance of running into an aggressive, warring race, with advanced technology. "You don't want to give away the motherland." Their roots come from a very old culture on a planet within the Orion system, which will go unnamed due to their desire for seclusion. There were also other smaller groups which inhabited islands here and there.

Once again, war broke out between Atlantis and Mu. The war was so devastating it disintegrated great cities and knocked the Earth off its axis, creating a polar shift approximately 10,500 years ago, as we mentioned earlier. The great city of Mu was destroyed by laser blasts, the intensity of which were so hot they melted the entire city, leaving it in complete ruin. There is a flat shelf underneath the sands in the Gobi desert, which is all that is left of the melted ruins of Mu.

The scientists of Mu, utilizing their great ships and latest technology, directed a meteor which targeted Atlantis.

The explosion was so great it actually knocked the Earth off its axis to its present position, causing the oceans in a great wave to scour the land. The heat generated from the explosion removed all traces of the once-great city of Atlantis, causing almost the entire continent to split and collapse beneath the waters. Nature took care of the rest.

The colonies went down with the great floods, land displacements and the shift of the axis, all due to war and the misuse of these energies. The air was filled with smoke and ash, and it took 50 years to settle. Some of their remains are still intact, buried as deep as 6,000 feet beneath the oceans. This will give you a clue as to how severe was the devastation.

There are literally thousands of extraterrestrial civilizations that have interacted in the past with Humanity and the Earth. Some took up residence and left many unexplained monuments behind as testimony to their advanced capabilities, which to this day cannot be duplicated.

The reason some of these ancient temples were so large is because those who built them, as ancient legends recall, were very tall. They came from much larger planets than Earth; hence they needed a larger body, which physically adapts to the environment. The stones were cut with laser light and levitated into place, which will answer the age-old question of how they were cut so precisely, and how they were lifted into place. To this day we do not have the technology or the equipment to duplicate them.

There have been great wars in the heavens that have crossed over into other galaxies, in which whole planets were blown to bits. Mars was once inhabited, and in a different orbit than today. There was even another planet called Melona in your solar system that preceded your present planet, and it was blown to bits. The asteroid belt and meteors are fragments of the remnants of Melona.

There have been planetary collisions and visiting comets and asteroids which have created havoc in your system. Venus is a newcomer to this system, and was dragged in by a great destroyer comet. You have had one moon, two moons; then there was no moon, and again one moon.

The history of UFOs far precedes time as you know it. There are advanced civilizations which existed billions of years before the Earth began its solidification into mass. Rather than attempt this arduous task, we will stick to Humanity's recorded history and time as you know it.

The first recorded encounters with UFOs go back to ancient Sumerian and Tibetan texts and the Bible. The Winged Gods, the fiery chariots, the viamanas, the Celestial Sons of God, the Celestial Boats that traversed the heavens, the Gods of thunder and fire on the mountaintops, the pillar clouds that were afire by night, and the clouds which many of your great masters were caught up or ascended into, all were recorded encounters with extraterrestrial beings.

Not all of these beings were benevolent, nor had Humanity's highest and best good in mind. In ancient times, it was as if two advanced travelers were to say, "Where do you want to go for lunch—how about dropping in on Earth for a rack of lamb, a flask of wine, and do the God thing?" Some of them made an extended vacation out of it. We are giving you a little extraterrestrial humor here (blasphemous as it may be) to lighten things up.

As Ezekiel, I recorded my encounter with Jehovah, an extraterrestrial who was technologically and mentally advanced, yet spiritually backward. He was the jealous, wrathful God, a merciless tyrant that destroyed village after village for not worshipping him and following his edicts.

His tyranny lasted thousands of years and was the origin of many misperceptions. The flashing lights in the firmament, the ship with bronze feet like calves, and the sound of a thousand rushing rivers were the landing of his ship. The smaller vehicles with wheels within wheels and flashing lights were referred to as cherubim.

When Jehovah ordered his men with their shattering weapons to destroy all the men, women and children of Israel, he prophesied that for 100 years anyone who came to

---

Israel would die a hideous death. Their hair and fingernails would fall out, and they would become food for the ravens and the beasts.

To ensure that his prophecy would come true, he had a man dressed in white linen (a radioactive protective garment) reach into the bowels of the cherubim and spread hot coals (radioactive material) around the city. He used his ship to blow entire cities off the face of the Earth that would not worship him and follow his edicts. This is one encounter that left a very deep scar upon the collective consciousness of Humanity concerning the nature of GOD.

Whenever you have a singular entity say he is GOD, he falls very short of omnipresence. If he was the totality of GOD, he would only be warring upon himself. A singular entity can become one with GOD, realizing there is no separation in omnipresence, yet there is a code of behavior that goes along with that union. Jehovah did not measure up to that code, for he arrogantly held himself separate and above Humanity. He demanded to be worshipped, and held Humanity in subservience. He was a mentally and technologically evolved merciless tyrant.

There are two other groups that came to Earth's rescue. They defeated Jehovah and chased what was left of his armada to the other end of the galaxy, where the remnants exist to this day. **Those who defeated Jehovah are known as the Pleiadians/Plejarans** (we will refer to them as the Pleiadians) **and the Andromedans,** who are known as the great guardians and overseers. They came upon the request and prayers of Yahweh, the God of love and peace, and The Great White Brotherhood, a collection of Ascended Masters who are here to this day upon the Earth.

The Andromedans are what Humanity has mythologically called the Archangels. They have the great ships which are domed triangles and black as the midnight sky. They can light up brighter than 10,000 suns. Michael, Gabriel, Rafael and a host of others are among them. It took only one of their ships, along with the Pleiadians, to send Jehovah packing.

The Andromedans are eight to ten feet tall and have magnetized light bodies. Genetically, Humanity resembles the Orions, Sirians, Pleiadians and the Andromedans (before their Ascension into light), more than any other races. In fact, you are a combination of their seed. Not only do you have a wonderful mixture of genetics from the stars, you also have the genetics from the Human experience evolving on Earth naturally.

Those who come from the heavens are your elder brothers. One of the reasons there is so much confusion on the Earth is because it is like a grand genetic experiment, in which the whole universe has stock. When you add your soul to the equation, it gets even more confusing, because many of you in your souls are from distant galaxies, and are often referred to as Star Seeds.

There is one thing in common you all have and that is life and the God seed, which is present within all of you. Activating that God seed creates a quickening, a physical transmutation bringing the body current with the God who resides within it. You lack for nothing, and in the light you are all equal, though genetically diverse.

Your heavenly brothers and sisters in the stars have been overseers of the evolution of Humanity, and have divinely intervened on many occasions on your behalf. It was often experienced as an act of Nature, so as not to create a lot of fear, superstition and worship that would interfere in evolution or distract one from finding the God within.

The remnants of the Jehovah group are still based upon the Earth. They always have been. Their effectiveness and control was greatly diminished with Jehovah's defeat.

Part of Jehovah's group did a lot of good for Humanity. They helped to instill moral codes of behavior, and resurrected dynasties out of lost, ignorant people. Because of this, they were allowed to stay. However, they had to discontinue with creating the images of Gods and demons to control and keep man in superstitious fear and ignorance. They have the ability to telepathically control people and place thoughts and visions in their heads to get them to do their bidding through a process called telenosis, a combination of telepathy and hypnosis. The part they have played in the history of Earth is beyond the comprehension of most, for they have controlled many of your key government and religious leaders at various times throughout history. They have been the inspiration behind the tyrants.

Even Hitler, who began with the most noble of intentions, fell under their control, along with those who surrounded him. Most of them have turned around, yet there is still a rebellion among a few of them who long for the days of old. They want to again be worshipped as Gods, controlling and manipulating Humanity. To this day, there are a few who are continuing to manipulate key officials within your religious and government institutions through telenosis.

Although they were deprived of most of their technology and their ships, **there are other scout ships returning to try to open the door for the return of Jehovah's lineage.** Their ships are red and green, but you won't see very many of them. Those who do come will be dropping from the heavens in fiery crashes, because they have failed to heed a very stern warning. Interfering in the awakening and healing of Humanity and the Earth and the divine right to free will and self-determination will no longer be tolerated.

Those who were telepathically controlling some of your key figures have recently been captured and removed from the Earth. Now Humanity can heal the controlling and destructive habits of the past without outer influences. Your government will be very busy cleaning up the messes of those in this group trying to return when their ships fall from the skies. It will be an impossible task in the future to hide the truth. The greater portion of Humanity already believes in UFOs and the government cover-up.

Another group which has received the most attention by Humanity is referred to as the Grays, or the Zetas. They come from a place referred to as Zeta Reticuli. They are the little people with big black eyes. Though short in stature, they are very powerful. They can alter time, distance and space, and are the ones responsible for all those abductions you have heard so much about. They can take you anywhere, anytime, have their way with you, and put you back without you even knowing.

They are very mentally and technologically advanced, and are millions of years old in time, as you know it. The smaller workers live to be 400 to 450 years old and are cloned. They are governed by a much larger group, similar yet taller in stature, which are ancient.

In their quest for knowledge above all else, they did away with emotions. This was their downfall, for now their entire race is dying. Love is the life force that sustains life. Without love the body withers to a very weak and somewhat useless vehicle. Why do you need a body if all you seek is a higher mind or intelligence?

They have to immobilize you and blank out your memory, because you are a fearful, warlike creature. With one blow you could crush them or easily break their arms and legs. You are unpredictable, and physically much more powerful. They have realized the error of abandoning the physical, and are genetically breeding emotions back into their civilization.

They are using the seed of Humanity to create a new hybrid which is half Earth Human, half Zeta. Those they chose to be part of their experiment are often very sensitive, very emotional, and often mystical in their beliefs concerning GOD and the universe. Their ships are rust or orange colored and burst into white light when traveling in high gear, so to speak. These ships are the ones that make the news, because of the extensive contact.

They have abducted millions and have been with Humanity for a very long time. Those they have chosen have a probe up their rectum, up their nose or deep within the ear, and often have scoop mark scars underneath, which are monitoring devices. They have been tagged and are monitored, just as you monitor many of your own wildlife upon

---

the Earth. They cherish life, honor the connectedness of all life, and are endeavoring to create a new life, a new beginning for their people. This has been allowed, and those who participate in this have a choice. They can see themselves as noble participants in saving an entire civilization, or helpless victims.

How individuals each choose to interpret the experience is up to them. If you act like a victim or act fearful and aggressive, you will be treated accordingly. They want to work with you, and speak with you on even ground.

They communicate telepathically. They do not speak. They don't have ears or a mouth, as you know it. They live off prana. They are the ones who have been experimenting on your cattle in order to better understand the reproductive system and the way animals on Earth assimilate energy through food and air. It is all foreign to them. If you think that is barbaric, visit one of your slaughter houses. The next time you bite into a burger, ask yourself just who is the barbarian.

In the past, they were unaware of the emotional trauma created during the abductions, mainly because they had no reference points concerning emotions. Only when their children began to display emotions did they begin to understand emotions, and they were quite perplexed. The children would cry, have wants, don't wants, likes, dislikes and want to be held, and they found it very confusing. It was almost more than they could handle; thus they had to get help. That is why the abduction story began to change, with humans often participating in holding and nurturing their children. This is all new to them.

They have the ability to create novas, engage matter beyond your wildest dreams, and alter time, distance and space with their own powerful consciousness. When it comes to emotions and attending to the needs of their children endowed with emotions, which they find completely illogical, they are in total confusion. It seems that rearing a child with emotions is a task beyond their abilities.

This may give many of you mothers out there a new perspective concerning your worth and capabilities. They hold you in high regard, and the Zetas, masters of the universe with their powerful consciousness and their very large heads, are learning from you.

Within the Zetas, there are subgroups. There are crossbreeds which are part Zeta, part Humanity; remember, this has been going on for hundreds of years. There are Zetas at different levels of consciousness or different stages of evolution. There are also workers which are nothing more than biological robots.

Just as Humanity has diversity in consciousness, other races also have the same diversity. If you were to go to another country and have a good or bad experience with an individual or a group within that country, it is inconsistent to judge the entire country based upon that experience. So goes the universe. Although there are collective agendas, there are also subgroups.

Your government is very aware of the Zetas. They have enough wreckage of UFOs to start their own UFO salvage and parts store, along with a working model. They even have a few unfortunate aliens on ice that died in various crash sites, and have also had a few live ones.

They have a lot of borrowed technology and have done a lot of back engineering to improve their own ships. They have known about the abductions and have traded knowledge with the Grays for quite some time. Their project Blue Book and other investigative agencies were not trying to prove UFOs exist—they already knew UFOs existed. They have well documented the existence of UFOs in what they refer to as their bible of flying saucers.

These agencies were created to spread disinformation, discredit any credible sightings, and to persuade people into believing they saw something other than the obvious. They were very good at it. There were a few who ended up in insane asylums, only because they were a witness to one of your government's secret experiments. They even went so far as to do a few lobotomies in the interest of national security.

They are the ones with the black unmarked helicopters filled with electronic surveillance gadgetry that scramble to areas where there is known UFO activity. They have their ground forces, which also in the name of national security deceive, harass and spy upon their own people, the people who are funding them, investing billions into their black projects, only to have their trust betrayed.

In the days to come, they will set up prominent investigators and scientists with photographs and tapes which are false, yet most of the information is true. They have the original tapes and photographs, but release the false ones with enough corresponding documentation to set the hook and then release the evidence later, proving it wrong, leaving everyone disappointed, with egg on their face and with no credibility.

The Roswell autopsy tapes are fabrications which fall into this arena. They went so far as to dissect a 16-year-old girl who died of a disfiguring disease to make it realistic enough to get top UFO investigators to stand behind it, and those who do will be in for a big surprise when they release the proof that it is a fake. All to cover up an event that really did happen. They have the real tape, the evidence and the bodies. They will spread a lot of disinformation concerning your benevolent brothers and sisters in the stars who are here to usher in a new age of enlightenment and the end of tyranny.

The government's agenda is to create one world government. To further their agenda, they will create the image of other-worldly threats to get governments and the people to unite, and go so far as to use the names of your benevolent brothers and sisters in the stars to be the ones threatening the Earth. Beware of them! They are very clever; yet in the long run, they will be the ones exposed in the end, for truth always comes forward.

If they were to invest those billions back into their own people and trust was restored, they would create a unified effort and gain even more information. If their intentions were directed towards the highest and best good of Humanity, there would be a grand reunion on a cosmic scale. There would be peace, unity and prosperity, not only for them, but for everyone.

The environment could also be restored very rapidly. They would gain all the knowledge and technology they desired. First they must have the consciousness before they can have the knowledge and technology. They sabotage their own desires in their lust for power and control, settling for far less.

They are the ones who have confiscated the technology taken from the Germans after World War II, who had been experimenting with their own ships which defied gravity. **The German scientists fled before things went bad in Germany and set up two bases: one in the Arctic and one in Brazil.** They continued to perfect their craft; and the old bell-shaped craft gave way to sleeker models which were wider and resembled more of what most believe a flying saucer would look like.

They and their families are there to this day, yet they have evolved further than most people, because their advent into the heavens brought them in contact with other advanced races. This contact has caused them to grow spiritually and technologically, because it is a prerequisite of advanced civilizations to balance spiritual evolution with technological evolution. It is very dangerous to grow in technology without spiritual wisdom; therefore technology is withheld until a high enough degree of spirituality is present. The Pleiadians come and go from these bases.

Your government has picked up the pieces at various extraterrestrial crash sites, including an alien ship that was only slightly damaged upon impact when the crew died due to a collision with a vehicle from another visiting race. They have built their own flying saucers which are bell-shaped, along with the newer disks. Compared to the interstellar and interdimensional ones, they are very primitive.

They even pose as extraterrestrial visitors on occasion. Their ships are dangerous, due to their radiation. Many have died accidentally from their emanations. There have been many explosions within your government's ships because of their instability, some of which is mistaken as other-worldly experiences.

When we say your government, we do not include all of your government. Your government consists of many different facets. You have the military, the elected officials and politicians, the CIA and the FBI, and the secret government.

The secret government is governed by the international bankers, and they are the ones behind the scenes, not only in this country, but in the rest of the world. They have their own people in key positions, who are informed only on a need-to-know basis. Not even your past Presidents had access to these black projects. They are the last word as to what is covered up in the name of national security and what is released.

Your government has also parlayed with the Pleiadians in the past; yet in their arrogance, they tried to entrap them, which was known far in advance by the Pleiadians, due to their telepathic abilities. Your government has met with and been denied access to those within your interior, and they have been tracking even the great ships coming from the Andromedas.

The group to which you have given your power to act upon your behalf concerning visitors from distant galaxies, your government, is very perplexed when it comes to communication with these other civilizations. They have scrambled from one contact to another, trying to gain information. In the past, they were in the dark concerning the nature of most other advanced civilizations and their intentions, mainly because of their own misguided intentions. They are baffled as to why they are not being contacted. After all, they represent the powers that be, and have scientists on hand, ready to make misuse of all their wonderful technology, incarcerate them, probe them, dissect them and ensure that they cannot return to their own people, their own families.

This is exactly why the contacts are happening with those with open minds, loving hearts and good intentions, rather than them. They do not have the consciousness necessary to engage spiritually and technologically advanced civilizations. This has recently changed. Your government, because of tumultuous times ahead, knows everything. They have been formally contacted, yet engaged as a hostile race for security measures and told of dire things in the days to come.

They have seen the cataclysms coming in the next years, and have been told there would be assistance on one condition—that they come clean and inform the people. **Your government has two options. One, keep quiet** and go into the secret underground facilities they have spent billions of your tax dollars creating, which are spread across the country, many of which will be submerged, defeating their purpose. **Or two, graciously accept the divine intervention,** figuring out a way to diplomatically break the news to the people that they have been deceiving for over 60 years, that cataclysmic changes are just around the corner. Which direction do you think they are going to take? Look at the past. It is a me-first organization.

The messages will be received by prophets and saints everywhere. No matter what choice they take, the truth will come forward, as truth always does. It is happening as we speak. There will be those who will turn a deaf ear to the prophecies and continue right up to the end times believing in the government's noble intentions and what social consciousness is telling them through the media. The last voice they will hear is, "This broadcast is permanently disrupted due to Nature. Don't bother tuning into another channel, because they are all gone."

The greatest of these spiritually and technologically advanced beings are the Andromedans. They are the great overseers. They understand why the changes are necessary; they know that you are eternal, and this is part of your evolution as well as the planet's need to rejuvenate herself. They are advising not to interfere, other than continuing to inspire from above.

Their ships are triangular, domed ships, which are black as the midnight sky. They have a white light on the bottom of each corner and a greater red light in the middle. The smaller ships of this group are about 100 yards long. The size of the mothership is beyond belief. It is a flying city.

Both are interstellar and interdimensional, and can be here one moment and across the universe in another moment. Your government sends their fighters up to engage them, and they disappear into another dimension or make right angle turns at several thousand miles an hour.

Fighters that get close enough find their systems fail long before they reach firing range, and have to turn back. Some have landed, only to find their weaponry had vanished or was completely disabled. There have been cases where fighter pilots have fired upon them point-blank with everything they had with no results, and were humiliated by the UFO's ability to outmaneuver them or lead them on a merry chase and just disappear.

Some of the fighters, along with their pilots, also just disappeared. You would think that by now the military would be humble enough to choose peace. They have chosen instead to build magnetic pulse generators, lasers and other new weapons to shoot them down. It's like going after a lion with a pea shooter: "Not very smart!"

The great ships can incinerate an entire planet in a moment, and it would be nothing, compared to their capabilities. Lucky for Earth they are understanding and benevolent. They were once just like Earth in their ancient history, though now are far beyond Earth in evolution. **If Humanity were to choose peace and cooperation, they would have an alliance of an Armada beyond belief**—one that is already working on behalf of Humanity, despite the continued efforts to war upon it.

This Armada of which we speak is one which has gone

to war on behalf of Humanity in the past, and is set up again to protect Humanity in what will be known as the last great war and end of Jehovah's lineage. They are here because of the psychical and psychological disease upon this plane and the Earth changes which are rapidly unfolding. They are very aware of the tyranny which has stunted the evolution of Humanity and is destroying the very platform for life, Earth.

They are also working arduously through the vibrational lifting and healing process, spiritually and technologically balancing out the energies and keeping the Earth's energy grid intact. They are working with many individuals upon the Earth, inspiring them and ushering in a higher awareness and new clean technology. That is how greatly you are loved, despite yourselves. It is as if the entire universe has come to watch and assist in the birth of Humanity and the Earth into a new time, a new consciousness and a new place in the universe.

The Pleiadians also are very involved in this process. The Pleiadian ships vary in size and color. They have small scout ships called telemeters, which are unmanned. These are silver and look like two pie pans, one on top of the other. They have another manned silver ship and a gold ship. Both look similar in shape, only the domes are taller on the top and bottom. They look more like a two-sided top, very similar to the metal ones you used to crank up and spin as a kid.

They also have larger star cruisers and motherships housing thousands, and in some cases millions. These are the ones that are appearing and disappearing in America, Switzerland, South America and other parts of the world. They can be physical or seen in the same shape as white light, depending on the frequency of their ship. They are the messengers. They are working with many, inspiring a more spiritual, rather than material, way of interacting with the Earth and each other. They are already based underground within Earth.

They also have a transfer station shared by others on

the dark side of the Moon, which, along with Mars, to this day has ancient ruins upon it. They have the great evacuation and colonization ships of their Lyrian forefathers, which have been refitted and upgraded, yet maintain their original shape and size.

At this point in time, for those who think they are going to be evacuated by these ships, don't count on it. Your planet and the tumultuous times ahead are a direct result of its inhabitants who are bent upon destroying not only themselves, but the very platform for life upon which they reside. Because of this, they have direct orders from a higher council not to interfere with your evolution and the lessons gained from the reactions to your actions.

The ancient ruins and the great ships will be revealed to the masses very soon in your future, much to the dismay of your government. Your brothers in the heavens will be making their presence known undeniably in your future.

Those within the interior will also be darting about your heavens, observing you and what you are doing to the environment. They have a shared equity in the water and air, and are very concerned about the nuclear testing. Their ships consist of pure plasma energy, merged with their own being, and are blue or white, depending upon their frequency, and they also have motherships.

Another group known as the Sirians is also very advanced. Their forefathers once colonized Earth and were known as the Black race. They are mentally and technologically highly evolved beings who do not understand the race discrimination so prevalent upon this planet. Many of them left before the cataclysms forced those remaining on Earth to start again as primitives.

They too are returning to lend a hand in saving a rebellious lot, some of whom would even discriminate against them. Their ships are often disk or golden egg shaped, emitting different colored lights depending upon their frequency or the speed at which they are traveling. They have other models as well.

There are also the remnants of the Lyrians, who are now peaceful and have ships which are also disk-shaped. There are the people from Arcturus, there are those from a parallel universe, and time travelers both from our future and from other galaxies.

There are the people from Orion, who are cousins of the Pleiadians. They have the same forefathers, and are just a little behind the Pleiadians in evolution. They have their disks, and one in particular looks strikingly similar to the ship on the new Star Trek Voyager.

As many have surmised, the many Star Trek series have been divinely inspired as an introduction to a greater reality with endless possibilities. There are billions of suns in your Milky Way alone with life-sustaining planets within their orbits. There are also civilizations upon many of them which have adapted to the various environments and are in different stages of evolution.

There are many other civilizations which have visited Earth. There are explorers who have ships which are very slow compared to most of the other ships in the universe. They have embarked upon journeys that have taken years to reach Earth, only to realize that you are very frightened, primitive people. They have walked among you, gathered data about your cultures and civilizations, the flora, animal life and geophysical data, and then they left.

There are even planets covered entirely by water, and aquatic humanoid life forms which are very advanced, with fish-like characteristics. If you were not so warlike and primitive, they would have shared information about their world and clean technology, which would solve many of your environmental problems.

There are those who came in what was perceived as a long, cylindrical white light. It was pure energy. There are also beings whose embodiments are adaptations to other very diverse planetary environments which, though very spiritually and technologically advanced, would provoke fear and mass hysteria if they were to land and walk among you.

They are waiting for you to get over your hang-ups on outer appearances. They also have their variety of ships. There will come a day when you will find that the imagination of many of your science fiction writers was not far from the truth. Many were drawing upon past life experiences.

The stars are filled with life. Even space is teaming with the building blocks of life, and some meteors and asteroids are full of the seeds of life. It is time to grow up and embrace all life with an open mind and a loving heart.

These understandings are given to prepare Humanity to take its rightful place in the universe. You could never be controlled, abducted or had your destiny interfered with if you were awake. Because of relying almost completely on your five senses and shutting down in consciousness from the great GOD of your origin, you can be controlled and manipulated—very easily, I might add. It is nothing to place a thought or experience telepathically in your mind, and it would be as real to you as if it really happened.

Those who are spiritually advanced never trespass on free will or interfere in your divine right to free will and self-determination. You must evolve naturally. That is why they stay hidden in the clouds, high in the heavens or within great mountains at another frequency. Though they are fully aware of you, they remain invisible to those who rely on only the five senses. They can make themselves fully visible to all your senses if you are ready and if you can greet them in love as equals.

They do not want to be worshipped. They do not want to be warred upon, though—it would be very unwise. They do not want to be feared and have you running to the mountains and hiding in caves. What they want is for you to drop the superstitious fears and dogmas and treat them as brothers. They want you to join them in peace and take your place alongside of them in the universe. That's what they want.

If you want to have a contact, you have to have the consciousness for it. If you act like a victim, the experience you have will be seen through the eyes of a victim. The experience, or lack thereof, is directly related to your consciousness. Consciousness creates reality on every level, every plane, every dimension. Call forward the God of your being and act accordingly. You will be greeted by the Gods and treated like a God, not one that has dominion over others, but one that loves and allows others, a loving, joyous, fearless entity. All you have to do is be yourself, your true self.

These spiritually and technologically advanced beings all agree: *If Humanity could end its warring, competitive behavior and learn to work together, in a very short time there would be an end to disease and poverty, the environment would be cleaned up, all your energy needs would be met with clean free energy, and you could take your place within the federation and begin to explore far off distant galaxies. It is not a very hard choice.*

On one hand, we have famine, plagues, social, economic and environmental collapse, with cataclysmic Earth changes; on the other, peace, unity, individual freedom and prosperity for everyone, not to mention a quantum leap in evolution and consciousness. Despite the obvious choice, there will be those who will wish to remain in control, due to vested interest, ignorance or not wanting to move out of their comfort zone.

We spoke earlier about an electrical band placed around the Earth, which is bringing balance back to this plane. Not only is the resonant frequency of Earth going to increase, the frequency of your bodies is going to increase as well. This is going to create a quickening and a quantum leap in evolution, despite those who are against it, for it is necessary if Humanity is to continue as a species, and it is an answer to the prayers of the majority. A civilization and a planet is a terrible thing to waste.

Humanity and the Earth will enter a new time flow. This is being brought about by the Beautiful Many Angelic Guides and Ascended Masters, the Constants, your beloved brothers living within the interior of your Earth and your beloved interdimensional brothers from distant galaxies.

There are also those living on the Earth, "the ground crew," who are also contributing their blessed consciousness and energy to the vibrational lifting and healing process. Unknown to many, there is much good done by these beloved entities. Be grateful.

An Andromedan Alternative

We spoke earlier about the Andromedans, yet we now desire to give you a little history concerning their interactions in the past with Earth and other civilizations throughout the universe.

The Andromedans are known as the great overseers (not overlords), because they understand the necessity for civilizations to evolve on their own. They also know that to do everything for you would create a dependency and devolution as well. It is like a child that is not challenged to figure out things for itself and do things for itself. It becomes very dependent, insecure and underdeveloped. It also lacks self-worth, because of its lack of ability to perform and create on its own. They do, however, intervene, just as a mother would when her child falls down or is in a life-threatening situation, such as the condition of your planet.

The Pleiadians are peaceful descendants of the Lyrians, who were very warlike conquerors that could not even get along with themselves. They often warred upon each other; and the colonization of the Pleiades, Orion and Haydes were due to people fleeing from such wars. These wars raged throughout the Galaxy.

To give you an understanding of how close this was to Earth, consider that Mars and another planet called Melona were devastated in these wars. Melona was blown to bits, the remnants of which are now your asteroids, and Mars was blown out of its cradle orbit, only to become a barren wasteland. They were both once beautiful planets, covered with life and inhabited. The Earth was still in its early stages of development and uninhabited, other than a few research facilities, which is why it was spared.

The warring continued in far off galaxies, followed by peace, until another tyrant came forward and gathered the scientists together with evil intentions, and in their lust for power, war again rocked the heavens. This continued until a great comet destroyed most of the Lyrians by almost completely devastating their homeland and another nearby planet they inhabited.

The Pleiades, Orion and Haydes were now the best hope for their people. Luckily, these three systems they inhabited were colonized by the peace lovers who fled the great wars. In their travels to far-off distant galaxies, they encountered a group of highly advanced beings in the Andromedas. These beings were more spiritual than physical, and their wisdom far surpassed the Pleiadians'. The Andromedans' technology and mastery over cosmic forces, and their great love for Humanity and all life humbled them, and they asked the Andromedans if they would lead them.

A high council was formed, consisting of Andromedans who would lead only by making suggestions. They had laws of their own they had to adhere to, and one of them was to honor the divine right to free will and self-determination of all people. They also knew, as mentioned before, that they could teach and inspire, yet could not interfere in the evolutionary process unless coming events would stop the evolutionary process. Such has been the case with Earth, for on many occasions they have divinely intervened to ensure the survival of Humanity and the continuation of the evolutionary process.

They are mythologically called the Archangels, because they are eight to ten feet tall and have bodies that consist of magnetized light. Michael, Gabriel and a host of others have played a very important part in your history. They are unique, yet one with GOD, and are often referred to as the Winged Gods. **What you would call a miracle would be child's play for them.**

A federation of planets, consisting of the colonized planets of Orion, Haydes, the Pleiades, Sirius and a host of other civilizations, joined under the guidance of the High Council of Andromedans, and peace flourished throughout the galaxies. Along with peace came a spiritual awakening within the cultures aligned with the federation, which became very prosperous and technologically advanced. Their spirituality gave them a greater understanding of the universe and forces within the universe. They want for nothing material, because their material needs are easily met.

What they quest for is knowledge, and they have dedicated themselves to assisting those of a lesser understanding to be all they can be. They, in turn, for the assistance granted to them by the Andromedans, wish to pass it along. They chose the assistance of the Andromedans, and are bound by the same universal principles which honor each individual's divine right to free will and self-determination.

It is up to the people of Earth to also choose. They will inspire and send their love, joy and wisdom to you, but the choice is up to you. **The Earth must unite.** There must be one world government—not governed by the ambitious ones who lust for power, but by the common people inspired by spiritual forces dedicated to the awakening and healing of all Humanity and the Earth.

Religions must also allow their names, images and doctrines to take a lesser priority, focusing more on goals and intentions. It is no longer appropriate to defend or war for the sake of names, images and doctrines, which have never been in the name of GOD, but in the desire for power.

Spirituality must also come into balance with materialism, which has been growing at a much faster rate, creating a serious imbalance, threatening all Humanity. It is the innermost desire of all Humanity to live a loving, joyous, prosperous life in peace and freedom. It is also Humanity's innermost desire to unite with their Creator—not some name or image far off in the ether which falls far short of omnipresence, but the God within them. These are the

God-given rights of all Humanity, and must be the goals and intentions of the governing forces. This is all being brought forward within the soul of each individual, along with individual freedom and power.

The Federation, along with the Andromedans, is bringing you a Higher Consciousness and Energy, as we speak. The tyrants will come forward in all walks of life, only to fall. Those who wish to dominate, control and manipulate, and those who continue in their unbridled greed and lust for power, will be made known. As power comes to them, it will amplify their behavior and accelerate the reactions to their actions. They shall fall upon their own swords.

> *The Federation, along with the Andromedans, is bringing to you a Higher Consciousness and Energy.*

The power is coming to the masses, who will awaken, rise up and reclaim their own individual sovereignty, power and their God-given rights. That which is out of alignment with love as the manifesting force behind all creation, and that which is out of balance and does not honor the inseparable oneness of GOD, Humanity and Nature as One will be no more.

There are several questions which will come forward in the hearts and minds of all Humanity, which are inspired by the Andromedans and the legions they inspire. Everyone will begin to contemplate, *"What if we laid down all of our names, images and doctrines and just chose love? Rather than conquering Nature, what if we just chose to work and flow with Nature, inheriting the very forces of Nature herself?*

"What if individuals each became sovereign unto themselves—would there be a need for borders, excessive governments and armies? What if we could all agree on certain

---

universal principles and unite as a planet to bring them into manifestation?

"What if we diverted most of our time, energy and resources to the innermost desire of all Humanity, which is to live a loving, joyous, abundant life in peace and freedom? What if we directed our energies and resources to the awakening and healing of Humanity and the Earth?

What if love was the manifesting force behind all creation? What would a civilization and a planet look like where love is the manifesting force behind all creation? To where would they advance? How far out into the universe would it take them?"

The meek shall inherit the Earth and the heavens. Those who have open minds and loving hearts will see grand things in the days to come. The words "It is finished" will ring in the minds of all Humanity. Finished will be the days of the tyrants. **The alternative to the tyrants is love, and those who choose a different alternative will leave this plane, never to return, for the Earth is evolving into another frequency.** This gives a whole new meaning to the words "Love it or leave it."

These are the options and the alternatives set into place and inspired by the very Source itself. The Andromedans, the Beautiful Many Angelic Guides, Ascended Masters, other spiritually and technologically advanced civilizations and Nature herself are assisting in this endeavor.

You are going to see more and more phenomena in the skies. There will be continuous sightings, as the ships make their appearances known. This will escalate. They will begin to position themselves around the planet.

There will be a great mothership from the Pleiades, along with Andromedan motherships strategically surrounding the Earth. There will be many comings and goings at that time. They will be set up for a great event. They will be great intimidators to the ignorant, and a Godsend to those in the know. They will decide at that time according to the consciousness upon this plane how much they will intervene. They are already having council concerning this matter. Between now and then we have a lot of work to do on every level.

Manifesting a Contact

Before running out and investing in all kinds of elaborate equipment or contacting your government to find out what it knows, there are a few things you need to know.

You already have all the equipment you need to manifest a contact. **Many of you are already being contacted, yet are not aware of it.** That ringing in your ears, the pressure on the top of your head, the sensations within what is referred to as your third eye, the crown of your head, and what many refer to as a heating up of the body for no apparent reason,

> *All the equipment you need to manifest a contact is already within you.*

or chills brought on by a transmission of consciousness and energy, are all manifestations of a contact.

Those vivid dreams of ships and strange encounters aboard them, missing time and extreme moments of ecstasy are also by-products of a contact. Some contacts in the past were very traumatic, due to the nature of the beings doing the contacting, their methods and their intentions.

Not all contacts have been desirable; yet again it all depends upon your consciousness as to how you interpret the experience and how you are treated. Self-authority is a prerequisite, and it helps to have an interdimensional mind.

All the equipment you need is within you—it just has to be turned on and tuned up. *The first contacts will be telepathically in consciousness. When you are ready, they will appear to you in the physical,* but not until you have the consciousness for it. There will be many sightings far off in the distance, and a few close ups by those who just happen to be in the right place at the right time, yet what you really want is conscious communication.

As far as going to your government, you are going to go nowhere. Their priorities and values, as well as their motives and intentions, are not in order. **The extraterrestrials who are spiritually and technologically advanced are also very telepathic.** They are very aware of the motives of your government, which would utilize their technology improperly.

Your government has spent millions of dollars on elaborate equipment, all to little or no avail. Did the thought ever occur to them that advanced beings some billions of years old in the time flow as you know it would not be using radio waves? Would they wait around hundreds of years to pick up your radio message when they travel beyond the speed of light into hyperlight and shift dimensions? They operate on light principles and beyond light, which is consciousness.

It stands to reason: If you want to communicate, it is going to be done through consciousness, and those with an interdimensional mind can contact them anywhere. **The advanced ones contact those who have strong emanations in consciousness. They know and can sense, spiritually and technologically, your state of awareness.**

They do not contact those who lust for power, those who are caught up in religious superstition or those who want to make a religion out of their people. They are contacting the meek—those with open minds and loving hearts who can engage them without fear and without worship, as equals.

The ones who are going to have the best contact are those who have the ability to travel in consciousness interdimensionally. Unfortunately, the Earth, due to the consciousness of those who govern you, is designated as a hostile planet. That is why there are so many contacts in the wilderness or in remote areas.

There are many hot spots in remote areas where there is a lot of activity, and going there is a very good start. When you get there, meditate on an image. I would suggest the triangle. Send the image out telepathically. Power it with love. They'll get it. See it going out into the universe and creating a direct line of communication from their ships to your third eye.

After you have visualized and established this link, offer an invitation and show them where you are. Visualize their ship coming down from the heavens, and act as if you were aboard, coming to Earth. See yourself entering your solar system with its yellow Sun. See the Earth in its orbit.

As you get closer, look down upon the continent where you are located. As you move towards that continent, see the State, and where you are located within that State. Visualize landmarks such as mountains and rivers, and see where you are located adjacent to these landmarks. Visualize the land around you and your house or location, as seen from the air. See them hovering over the area, or landing, if you feel you are ready for it consciously. Live the experience as if it already happened. Embrace it emotionally, and you will draw to you the experience.

If it doesn't manifest right away, remember: They too have free will and an agenda. They are very busy doing their part in the universal scheme of things. The timing may not be right. Do not get disappointed or give up, thinking you are unworthy, they do not exist, or you are out of your mind. Keep trying.

If the ETs can't make it physically, they will often send you their blessings telepathically. I might add, they also have a wonderful sense of humor, and joy is one of the highest vibrational thoughts in the universe. Have fun with it.

> *If the ETs can't make it physically, they will often send you their blessings telepathically.*

In Conclusion

So you have finished the second stretch. These truths, outrageous as they may seem, are all a by-product of Inter-dimensional Mind, something you all possess. You only have to awaken to your Divinity, your true nature, which is a multidimensional being.

You are an eternal spirit, capable of going backward and forward in time and recalling all of your past life experiences in the eternal scheme of things. You are not bound by time, distance and space. You are capable of traveling from the beginning to the end, to other planes, dimensions and universes, and returning back to your little third dimensional body on a planet known as the plane of demonstration, the action/reaction world called Earth.

It is a place where the forgotten Gods reside, many of whom are asleep and have chosen a personality with all of its erroneous beliefs and a body as their only identity. You have been loved and allowed to do so, due to a divine right to free will and self-determination, and the unconditionally loving nature of creation.

You have come to a point in evolution where divine intervention is necessary to ensure the continuation of not only yourselves as a species, but your planet as well. Thus, the awakening and healing process has begun. It is not being done *to* you or necessarily *for* you; it is being done *through* you.

The God within you is coming forward. You all have your part, and a mission to accomplish. Each in your own unique way has a contribution to make and must move forward and create the necessary alignment with your soul and its purpose. This may or may not have anything to do with one's present position, yet you will find that your whole life up to now has been in preparation for this event.

There has been purposeful good in everything, and it's time to use the wisdom gained in each experience to help you accomplish your goals. Be sure your goals are in alignment with your soul's purpose and not the programming of social consciousness, and all will go well.

The information that has been given within this book is to bring you current and prepare you for a grand reunion. The Gods of old were your ancient ancestors, advanced forms of Humanity from other worlds, which descended from Heaven. They sat with your forefathers, took wives, feasted and played some very important roles in your history. Some served Humanity, and some demanded to be served by Humanity.

> *The information given within this book is to bring you current and prepare you for a grand reunion.*

Those who interacted in a negative way have long since evolved beyond interfering with primitive cultures and are now operating under what is known to you as the Prime Directive—a policy of noninterference with the evolution of planets and their inhabitants until they too are consciously aware as a collective that the universe is filled with intelligent life, and begin their journey into space.

You are genetically diverse Star Seeds which have evolved through thousands of years to a point where you are ready to reunite, not only with your ancient ancestors in the stars and on other planes and dimensions, but with the God of your being. The entire Earth is rising rapidly into a higher frequency from a base resonance of 7 megahertz to 12. Your bodies are following suit, which includes your subtle bodies as well.

Everything which does not align with the new Higher Consciousness and Energy is surfacing. Attitudes, emotions and actions which are not in the highest and best good for Humanity and the Earth and which do not align with the

---

laws of creation will no longer be appropriate. The manifestation process and the reaction time to actions are being greatly amplified and accelerated.

Truth will come forward in every arena. The days of denial and deception are fast coming to a close, as well as the end of the tyrants. You are entering exciting times of tumultuous social, economic and physical Earth changes. This understanding is necessary to prepare the way.

Enlightenment means to be enlightened of the whole story, both sides of the coin. **You must know where you have been to understand who you are and where you are going.** It is the past which has made you what you are today; and knowledge of the past, your true heritage, will break the spell and allow the memories to come forward like a mighty river. **Let go of that which no longer serves you, that which has become a burden and that which does not bring you joy.**

Align yourself with that which is a service rather than a disservice to Humanity and Nature. Live for the spirit within you. Honor your feelings, for GOD is a feeling, and act upon those feelings.

You have chosen these exciting times. Go forward in love, joy and freedom. See the God within all Humanity and Nature, and open up to even grander realities. The universe is the playground of an enlightened one. Come join us. If you need a little help, ask!

I LOVE YOU; that is all.

Be kind to others and the Earth.

Bring no harm to anyone or anything.

It's that simple!

Becoming Gods

Appendix

Bio of James Gilliland

James Gilliland is a minister, counselor, an internationally known lecturer, best selling author with the books, Reunion with Source, Becoming Gods, and The Ultimate Soul Journey. James appeared in Contact Has Begun, His Story, The History Channel, UFOs then and Now, UFO Hotspots, ABC, Fox News, BBC Danny Dyer Special, Paranormal State, ECETI Ranch a Documentary, and the new movie Thrive have all featured James and ECETI which he is the founder.

He has appeared on Coast to Coast, Jeff Rense, and to numerous other radio shows to mention also being the host of, As You Wish Talk Radio, www.bbsradio.com and Contact Has Begun, www.worldpuja.net. He is a facilitator of many Eastern disciplines, a visionary dedicated to the awakening and healing of Humanity and the Earth and teaches higher dimensional realities from experience.

For other books by James, DVD's, conferences, updates and more go to www.eceti.org